BEST-EVER
VEGETARIAN

BEST-EVER
VEGETARIAN

DELICIOUS MEAT-FREE DISHES FOR EVERY OCCASION: 150 IRRESISTIBLE
RECIPES SHOWN IN 250 STUNNING PHOTOGRAPHS

EDITED BY EMMA SUMMER

HERMES
HOUSE

This edition is published by Hermes House, an imprint of Anness Publishing Ltd, Blaby Road, Wigston, Leicestershire LE18 4SE
Email: info@anness.com

Web: www.hermeshouse.com; www.annesspublishing.com

If you like the images in this book and would like to investigate using them for publishing, promotions or advertising, please visit our website www.practicalpictures.com for more information.

Publisher: Joanna Lorenz
Editor: Daniel Hurst
Designer: Nigel Partridge
Proofreading Manager: Lindsay Zamponi
Editorial Reader: Lauren Taylor
Production Controller: Wendy Lawson

ETHICAL TRADING POLICY
At Anness Publishing we believe that business should be conducted in an ethical and ecologically sustainable way, with respect for the environment and a proper regard to the replacement of the natural resources we employ.

As a publisher, we use a lot of wood pulp in high-quality paper for printing, and that wood commonly comes from spruce trees. We are therefore currently growing more than 750,000 trees in three Scottish forest plantations: Berrymoss (130 hectares/320 acres), West Touxhill (125 hectares/305 acres) and Deveron Forest (75 hectares/185 acres). The forests we manage contain more than 3.5 times the number of trees employed each year in making paper for the books we manufacture.

Because of this ongoing ecological investment programme, you, as our customer, can have the pleasure and reassurance of knowing that a tree is being cultivated on your behalf to naturally replace the materials used to make the book you are holding.

Our forestry programme is run in accordance with the UK Woodland Assurance Scheme (UKWAS) and will be certified by the internationally recognized Forest Stewardship Council (FSC). The FSC is a non-government organization dedicated to promoting responsible management of the world's forests. Certification ensures forests are managed in an environmentally sustainable and socially responsible way. For further information about this scheme, go to www.annesspublishing.com/trees

NOTES
Bracketed terms are intended for American readers.

For all recipes, quantities are given in both metric and imperial measures and, where appropriate, measures are also given in standard cups and spoons. Follow one set, but not a mixture, because they are not interchangeable.

Standard spoon and cup measures are level. 1 tsp = 5ml, 1 tbsp = 15ml, 1 cup = 250ml/8fl oz

Australian standard tablespoons are 20ml. Australian readers should use 3 tsp in place of 1 tbsp for measuring small quantities.

American pints are 16fl oz/2 cups. American readers should use 20fl oz/2.5 cups in place of 1 pint when measuring liquids.

Electric oven temperatures in this book are for conventional ovens. When using a fan oven, the temperature will probably need to be reduced by about 10–20°C/20–40°F. Since ovens vary, you should check with your manufacturer's instruction book for guidance.

The nutritional analysis given for each recipe is calculated per portion (i.e. serving or item), unless otherwise stated. If the recipe gives a range, such as Serves 4–6, then the nutritional analysis will be for the smaller portion size, i.e. 6 servings. The analysis does not include optional ingredients, such as salt added to taste.

Medium (US large) eggs are used unless otherwise stated.

Main front cover shows Thai Yellow Vegetable Curry – for recipe, see pages 146–7

Contents

Introduction

The vegetarian diet offers a healthy and ethically sound approach to eating, and the many flavours, colours and textures that are integral to meat-free cooking open up a new world of food to the budding vegetarian chef, and offer a unique access point into many of the world's finest cuisines.

Some of the most exciting and innovative food available today is vegetarian. Glorious colours and enticing flavours epitomize this type of cooking, and when you consider the superb soups, appetizers, snacks, salads and main courses that make up green cuisine, it seems almost inconceivable that vegetarian food could ever have been considered dull or unappetizing.

When it comes to vegetarian cooking, the pleasure starts long before the cook reaches the kitchen. What could be more satisfying than stooping to pick fresh herbs, bruising them between the fingers and releasing their wonderful scents? Or meandering through a market, filling a basket with dark purple aubergines (eggplants), fat red tomatoes, glossy peppers, tiny radishes or creamy bulbs

of fennel with their feathery fronds? Shopping for spices is another delight, as is discovering a new type of oil or vinegar, or a supplier of fresh pasta.

Vegetarian food has come a long way from the dreary days when it had a reputation for being brown and beany. It may once have been marginalized, but today it is very definitely mainstream. Visit any good restaurant, especially at lunchtime, and many of the most delectable items on offer will be meat-free. Chargrilled slices of aubergine or courgette (zucchini), layered with goat's cheese and served with a rich tomato sauce, pasta with pesto and pine nuts, puff pastry parcels filled with baby vegetables, asparagus risotto – such delicious dishes are not on the menu because they are vegetarian, but because they are what people really love to eat.

The good news is that you don't have to go to a restaurant to taste treats like these. There are more than 150 wonderful vegetarian dishes in this collection, each one as appealing to the eye as the palate. Many of the dishes will naturally promote good health, but that's a bonus, not a

LEFT: *The vegetarian diet is naturally healthy, but also provides a plethora of exciting flavours and textures.*

ABOVE: *Vegetarian food offers a gateway into some of the world's best-loved cuisines.*

ABOVE: *Vibrant fruit and vegetables are a treat for the eyes as well as the taste buds.*

ABOVE: *Vegetarian cooking makes the most of fresh, seasonal ingredients.*

basic requirement. You'll find the frivolous and indulgent as well as the sane and sensible, so if you start a meal with cocktails and naughty nibbles, you can pick a healthy main course, such as the Aubergine Salad with Tahini Dressing or the Tagine of Butter Beans, Cherry Tomatoes and Olives. A balanced diet is not difficult to achieve. Try to eat plenty of fruit and vegetables, pulses, nuts, seeds, rice, bread, pasta and potatoes, with some dairy food or non-dairy alternatives.

With so many recipes to choose from, special-occasion cooking need never be a worry for vegetarians. There are elegant and delicious dishes for every occasion, such as Spaghetti with Wild Asparagus; Butternut Squash with Caramelized Pink Shallots; Smoked Aubergines in Cheese Sauce; or Pumpkin, Rosemary and Chilli Risotto. If you are looking to expand your culinary horizons, choose fragrant and exotic dishes from many of the world's best-loved cuisines, including China, India, Greece, Thailand, Italy and Morocco.

It is likely that as many non-vegetarians as vegetarians will enjoy this book. If you are a carnivore cooking for a vegetarian, it is essential to follow the recipes scrupulously, avoiding not only the obvious things, such as meat, poultry and fish, but also any products that may contain derivatives of these foods, such as fish sauce or Worcestershire sauce (of which there are vegetarian versions).

A number of the recipes feature cheese. We haven't stipulated vegetarian cheeses, assuming that committed vegetarians will choose varieties they feel able to use, while vegans will opt for recipes that exclude dairy products entirely. Although specific cheeses are listed in ingredients, it is almost always possible to substitute alternatives, just so long as you match like with like. A vegetarian Cheddar won't give you the same results as Parmesan, for instance, but the outcome will be perfectly acceptable.

Soup

Warm and comforting or cool and refreshing, a soup can be an elegant opener to a sophisticated dinner or a substantial meal in its own right. This chapter presents a variety of vegetarian soups that will suit all occasions and appetites, from traditional classics such as Potato and Leek Soup, through to more exotic but equally delicious offerings like Pumpkin, Snake Bean and Bamboo Soup with Coconut.

Cold summer soup

This elegant cold soup is perfect for serving as a light lunch or appetizer on a hot summer day. The refreshing combination of cucumber, fennel, celery and lettuce is enhanced with the robust flavours of tomato, basil, garlic and chilli to create an exciting and delicious result.

SERVES 6

1/2 cucumber, peeled and cubed
1 fennel bulb, thinly sliced
1 celery heart, chopped
1 lettuce, chopped
4 tomatoes, peeled, seeded and chopped
3 carrots, quartered
1 lemon, peeled and thinly sliced
3 garlic cloves, chopped
1 dried red chilli, finely chopped
1 bunch fresh basil
75ml/2¹/₂ fl oz/¹/₃ cup extra virgin olive oil
sea salt and ground black pepper
croûtons, to serve (optional)

1 Place the cucumber, slices of fennel, chopped celery, lettuce, tomatoes, carrots, lemon, garlic, chilli and basil in the bowl of a food processor, and gradually process all ingredients until well mixed. Alternatively, use a blender and blend until smooth.

2 Add 250ml/8fl oz/1 cup water and the extra virgin olive oil, then season with salt and black pepper to taste.

3 Ladle into a serving bowl and chill until required. Serve with croûtons, if you like.

Nutritional information per portion: Energy 119kcal/494kJ; Protein 1.3g; Carbohydrate 7.2g, of which sugars 6.9g; Fat 9.7g, of which saturates 1.4g; Cholesterol 0mg; Calcium 33mg; Fibre 2.9g; Sodium 23mg.

Tomato and bread soup

This is a very thick soup, which makes the best of the glut of overripe tomatoes at the end of summer. These are combined with that ever-present standby ingredient: stale bread. It is marvellous served lukewarm with plenty of basil and extra olive oil to drizzle over it.

SERVES 6

1.5 litres/2½ pints/6¼ cups vegetable, chicken or meat stock

1 large onion, chopped

1.2kg/2½lb very ripe tomatoes, coarsely chopped

120ml/4fl oz/½ cup extra virgin olive oil

400g/14oz stale ciabatta, crusts removed, thinly sliced

3 garlic cloves, crushed

a large handful of fresh basil leaves, chopped

sea salt and ground black pepper

1 Heat the stock gently in a large pan. Meanwhile, put the onion, tomatoes and half the oil in a separate pan and fry together over a gentle heat for 10 minutes, or until softened.

2 Push the onion and tomato mixture through a food mill or sieve (strainer) and add it to the hot stock. Stir thoroughly.

3 Add the bread, garlic and most of the basil, and season to taste.

4 Cover the soup and leave it to simmer for 45 minutes, or until thick and creamy, stirring occasionally.

5 Stir in the remaining oil, adjust the seasoning if necessary, and add the rest of the basil to taste. Serve hot or at room temperature.

Nutritional information per portion: Energy 285kcal/1194kJ; Protein 5g; Carbohydrate 28g, of which sugars 7.2g; Fat 17.9g, of which saturates 2.5g; Cholesterol 0mg; Calcium 64mg; Fibre 2.6g; Sodium 243mg.

Minestrone with marinated fried tofu

The addition of tofu makes this satisfying and appealing soup a meal in itself, which can be adapted to contain whatever vegetables are available. It is especially tasty if it is made with fresh seasonal produce, but can also be made with frozen mixed vegetables if needed.

SERVES 6

15ml/1 tbsp olive oil
2 leeks, finely chopped
2 celery sticks, finely diced
2 garlic cloves, finely chopped
2 courgettes (zucchini), finely diced
450g/1lb carrots, finely diced
200g/7oz green beans, finely sliced
5ml/1 tsp dried Mediterranean herbs
1.2 litres/2 pints/5 cups vegetable stock
400g/14oz can chopped tomatoes
300g/11oz marinated deep-fried
   tofu pieces
20g/¾oz bunch flat leaf parsley or
   basil, chopped
sea salt and ground black pepper

1 Preheat the oven to 200°C/400°F/Gas 6. Heat the oil in a large pan then sauté the leeks, celery and garlic for 7–8 minutes, or until softened and beginning to turn golden.

2 Add the other vegetables and dried herbs. Stir to mix well, then pour over the vegetable stock and canned tomatoes. Bring to the boil, then simmer for 20–25 minutes, until the vegetables are tender.

3 Meanwhile, place the tofu pieces on a baking sheet and bake for 8–10 minutes to warm through.

4 Add the chopped parsley or basil to the soup and season to taste with sea salt and pepper. Stir in the warmed tofu and serve immediately sprinkled with a grinding of extra black pepper.

Nutritional information per portion: Energy 122Kcal/510kJ; Protein 7.6g; Carbohydrate 12.2g, of which sugars 10.8g; Fat 5.1g, of which saturates 0.8g; Cholesterol 0mg; Calcium 328mg; Fibre 5.2g; Sodium 36mg.

Leek soup with feta, dill and paprika

Flavoured with dill and topped with crumbled white cheese, this creamy leek soup is warming and satisfying. The saltiness of feta is good in this soup, but you could just as well use Roquefort or Parmesan, both of which are equally salty. Serve with chunks of fresh, crusty bread.

SERVES 3–4

30ml/2 tbsp olive or sunflower oil

3 leeks, trimmed, roughly chopped
    and washed

1 onion, chopped

5ml/1 tsp sugar

1 bunch of fresh dill, chopped, with a few
    fronds reserved for the garnish

300ml/$\frac{1}{2}$ pint/1$\frac{1}{4}$ cups milk

15ml/1 tbsp butter (optional)

115g/4oz feta cheese, crumbled

salt and ground black pepper

paprika, to garnish

1 Heat the oil in a heavy pan and stir in the chopped leeks and onion. Cook for about 10 minutes, or until the vegetables are soft.

2 Add the sugar and chopped dill, and pour in 600ml/1 pint/2$\frac{1}{2}$ cups water. Bring to the boil, lower the heat and simmer for about 15 minutes.

3 Leave the liquid to cool a little, then process in a blender until smooth. Return the puréed soup to the pan, pour in the milk and stir over a gentle heat until it is hot. Don't let it come to the boil.

4 Season with salt and pepper, bearing in mind that the feta is salty. If using the butter, drop it on to the surface of the soup and let it melt.

5 Ladle the soup into bowls and top with the crumbled feta. Serve immediately, garnished with a little paprika and the dill fronds.

Nutritional information per portion: Energy 203kcal/844kJ; Protein 10g; Carbohydrate 10.9g, of which sugars 9.4g; Fat 13.5g, of which saturates 5.7g; Cholesterol 25mg; Calcium 259mg; Fibre 4.1g; Sodium 454mg.

Onion and beer soup

This delicious soup of caramelized onions and malty beer is the ultimate comfort food, and perfect for a cold winter's day. If you are feeling truly decadent, try topping the soup with a thin slice of toasted French bread, sprinkling generously with Gruyère and grilling the soup for 5–10 minutes until golden; the result will be gooey, fragrant and irresistible.

SERVES 4–6

50g/2oz/¼ cup butter

4 medium onions, (total weight about 800g/13/4lb), chopped

4 garlic cloves, finely chopped

1 medium potato (about 200g/7oz), peeled and chopped

45ml/3 tbsp sherry or Calvados (if not using beer – see below)

1 litre/1¾ pints/4 cups vegetable stock, or half stock and half beer

1–2 sprigs fresh thyme

1 bay leaf

salt and ground black pepper, to taste

45ml/3 tbsp chopped parsley, to garnish

freshly grated Gruyère cheese (optional)

hearty country bread or croûtons, to serve

1 Melt the butter in a large, heavy pan and sauté the onions over a medium-high heat for about 10 minutes or until lightly caramelized. Add the garlic and sauté for 1 minute more.

2 Add the potato to the onions and stir well. If you are using sherry or Calvados instead of beer, add it to the pan at this point and let the mixture simmer for 3 minutes more.

3 Pour in the stock (or stock and beer) and add the thyme and bay leaf. Bring to the boil, reduce the heat and simmer for 35 minutes.

4 Remove the herbs and purée with a hand-held blender or in a food processor, until it reaches the desired consistency.

5 Season with salt and black pepper, to taste. Reheat if necessary, then ladle the soup into bowls.

6 Top each serving with freshly chopped parsley and add the grated cheese, if you like. Serve immediately with hearty country bread or croûtons.

Nutritional information per portion: Energy 146kcal/608kJ; Protein 2.5g; Carbohydrate 16.3g, of which sugars 8.1g; Fat 7.5g, of which saturates 4.4g; Cholesterol 18mg; Calcium 38mg; Fibre 2.2g; Sodium 339mg.

Asparagus soup

This soup is best enjoyed in early summer when asparagus is abundant. The delicate flavour of the asparagus is enriched to a sumptuous, velvety texture by the butter and cream, and adding an additional swirl of cream to each bowl before serving makes this a very elegant soup indeed.

SERVES 4

500g/1¼lb white asparagus, peeled
   and trimmed
1.2 litres/2 pints/5 cups vegetable stock
   or water
65g/2½oz/5 tbsp butter
75g/3oz/⅔ cup plain (all-purpose) flour
120ml/4fl oz/½ cup whipping cream
salt and ground white pepper
finely chopped fresh parsley, to garnish

1 Cut the asparagus spears into 5cm/2in pieces and set the tips aside in some cold water.

2 Bring the stock or water to the boil in a pan, add the pieces of asparagus stalk and simmer for 20 minutes. Remove the asparagus with a slotted spoon and press through a sieve (strainer) into a bowl or process in a blender until you have a smooth purée. Reserve the stock.

3 Melt the butter in a large pan over a low heat, but do not let it brown.

4 Stir in the flour and cook, stirring constantly, for 2 minutes. Gradually stir in the stock, then add the asparagus purée and the cream.

5 Strain the soup into a clean pan, then return to the heat and bring to the boil, stirring constantly.

6 Drain the asparagus tips, add them to the soup and simmer, stirring occasionally, for 10 minutes, until they are tender. Season the soup with salt and pepper and serve immediately, garnished with chopped parsley.

Nutritional information per portion: Energy 331kcal/1368kJ; Protein 6.1g; Carbohydrate 18g, of which sugars 3.6g; Fat 26.5g, of which saturates 16.2g; Cholesterol 66mg; Calcium 80mg; Fibre 2.7g; Sodium 108mg.

Green bean and cabbage soup

This light and healthy summer soup owes much of its distinctive flavour to the addition of summer savory, with its aromatic, pungent flavour. Summer savory has a natural affinity with all kinds of beans, and is also said to help aid digestion.

SERVES 4

500g/1¼lb floury potatoes,
  cut into pieces
2 onions, chopped
300g/11oz Savoy cabbage
300g/11oz green beans, cut into
  1cm/½in lengths
1 small bunch of fresh summer
  savory, chopped
50ml/2fl oz/¼ cup olive oil
salt

1 Put the potatoes and onions in a large pan, add 1 litre/1¾ pints/ 4 cups water and bring to the boil. Cover and simmer over a gentle heat for about 20 minutes, until the potatoes are tender.

2 Transfer the potatoes, onions and cooking liquid to a food processor or blender and process to a purée. Return to the rinsed-out pan.

3 Cut the cabbage in quarters, cut out the core and slice in 2.5cm/ 1in pieces. Add the cabbage, the beans and summer savory to the pan and cook over a medium heat for a few minutes, until the cabbage is cooked, and the beans are tender but still slightly crisp.

4 Season with salt to taste, stir in the olive oil and serve immediately.

Nutritional information per portion: Energy 239kcal/998kJ; Protein 6.2g; Carbohydrate 34.2g, of which sugars 11.7g; Fat 9.6g, of which saturates 1.4g; Cholesterol 0mg; Calcium 96mg; Fibre 6.1g; Sodium 20mg.

Broad bean soup

This soup is both warming and hearty, and makes the most of the delightful combination of broad beans and distinctive summer savory. It is especially rewarding when served with a herby potato cake, making it an ideal option for a healthy and filling lunch or a light supper.

SERVES 4

2 onions

1 leek

1 celery stick

1 carrot

1 bay leaf

3 sprigs of fresh thyme

1 sprig of fresh rosemary

1.2–1.6kg/2½–3½lb shelled broad
   (fava) beans

1 bunch of spring onions
   (scallions), diced

30ml/2 tbsp cornflour (cornstarch)

1 bunch of parsley, chopped

salt

single (light) cream, to serve

FOR THE POTATO CAKE

500g/1¼lb potatoes, peeled

2 eggs, lightly beaten

pinch of freshly grated nutmeg

30ml/2 tbsp finely chopped fresh
   summer savory

25g/1oz/2 tbsp butter

salt and ground black pepper

1 Roughly chop the onions, leek, celery and carrot and place in a pan with the bay leaf, thyme, rosemary and a pinch of salt. Pour in 1.5 litres/2½ pints/6¼ cups water and bring to the boil, then lower the heat to a gentle simmer and leave for 30 minutes.

2 To make the potato cake, rinse the potatoes and dry on kitchen paper. Coarsely grate them into a bowl, stir in the eggs, nutmeg, and savory and season.

3 Melt half the butter in a 20cm/8in diameter non-stick frying pan. Scoop the potato mixture into the pan, pressing it out evenly with a fish slice or metal spatula, and cook over a low heat until the top is dry. Loosen the edges with a knife, if necessary, and turn the cake out on to a plate.

4 Melt the remaining butter in the pan, slide the cake back into it, the cooked side uppermost, and cook until browned on the underside. Keep warm over a very low heat.

5 Strain the stock through a sieve or colander. Discard the vegetables and return the liquid to the pan. Add the beans to the pan and cook for 15–20 minutes, until tender.

6 Remove half the beans from the soup and process in a food processor or blender. Stir the bean purée into the soup with the spring onions and cook for 2 minutes. Mix the cornflour to a paste with 60ml/4 tbsp water in a bowl and stir into the soup, cooking for a short time to thicken.

7 Season to taste with salt, sprinkle with the parsley and serve the soup with the potato cake and a jug (pitcher) of cream.

Nutritional information per portion: Soup per portion Energy 428kcal/1793kJ; Protein 46g; Carbohydrate 26.2g, of which sugars 5.1g; Fat 16g, of which saturates 5.2g; Cholesterol 46mg; Calcium 108mg; Fibre 9.2g; Sodium 1777mg.
Potato cake per portion: Energy 173kcal/ 727kJ; Protein 5.5g; Carbohydrate 20.4g, of which sugars 1.8g; Fat 8.4g, of which saturates 4.2g; Cholesterol 108mg; Calcium 38mg; Fibre 1.6g; Sodium 89mg.

Chervil soup

The addition of chervil gives a subtle aniseed flavour to this delicate soup, which is an ideal introduction to an elegant dinner. If you would like a slightly creamier texture, mix the chervil leaves with 60ml/4 tbsp crème fraîche before adding them to the soup.

SERVES 4

25g/1oz/2 tbsp butter

1 onion, finely chopped

1 leek, white part only, finely chopped

1 large potato, peeled and chopped

1 litre/1¾ pints/4 cups hot
    vegetable stock

stems and leaves from 1 bunch fresh
    chervil (about 150g/5oz), chopped and
    kept separate, plus a few chervil sprigs
    for the garnish

50g/2oz/½ cup cooked white long
    grain rice

salt and ground white pepper

1 Melt the butter in a large pan over a medium to high heat. Add the onion and sauté for about 5 minutes until fragrant and translucent.

2 Add the leek and potato and sauté, stirring constantly, for 5 minutes more.

3 Pour in the vegetable stock. Add the chopped chervil stems, bring to the boil, reduce the heat and simmer for 20 minutes or until the potatoes are tender. Add salt and pepper to taste.

4 Using a hand-held blender, food processor or a food mill, purée the soup until smooth. Stir in the chopped chervil leaves and cooked rice. Ladle into warm soup bowls and serve garnished with the chervil sprigs.

Nutritional information per portion: Energy 137kcal/573kJ; Protein 3.5g; Carbohydrate 17.6g, of which sugars 3.7g; Fat 6.3g, of which saturates 3.4g; Cholesterol 13mg; Calcium 98mg; Fibre 3.8g; Sodium 59mg.

Watercress soup

Watercress and garden cress are commercially produced to accommodate year-round demand, which means that the delicious peppery flavour of this moreish soup can be enjoyed whatever the season. This is a delicious and vibrant appetizer for a sophisticated meal.

SERVES 4

25g/1oz/2 tbsp unsalted butter
   or vegetable oil
1 large onion, chopped
1 leek, white part only, chopped
1 garlic clove, roughly chopped
2 large potatoes, peeled and cubed
1.5 litres/2½ pints/6¼ cups hot
   vegetable stock
1 bay leaf
1 large bunch of watercress, well rinsed,
   large stems removed, roughly chopped
1 large bunch of garden cress, well rinsed,
   large stems removed
salt and ground black pepper to taste
60ml/4 tbsp watercress leaves,
   to garnish

1 Heat the butter or oil in a large pan over a medium-high heat. Stir in the onion, then sauté for 2–3 minutes. Add the leek, garlic and potatoes. Sauté for 5 minutes more, stirring until the mixture becomes fragrant.

2 Pour in the vegetable stock and add the bay leaf. Bring to the boil, reduce the heat to medium-low, cover and simmer for 20–30 minutes, until the potatoes are tender.

3 Stir in the watercress and garden cress. Simmer uncovered, for 3 minutes and no longer, to cook lightly and preserve the fresh green colour.

4 Remove the bay leaf. With a hand-held blender or in a food processor, purée the soup until smooth or until it reaches the desired consistency. Season to taste with salt and pepper and reheat if necessary.

5 Ladle into warm bowls and serve, garnished with fresh watercress leaves.

Nutritional information per portion: Energy 598kcal/2515kJ; Protein 19.9g; Carbohydrate 76.3g, of which sugars 14.3g; Fat 25.9g, of which saturates 14.5g; Cholesterol 53mg; Calcium 602mg; Fibre 13.7g; Sodium 348mg.

Potato and leek soup

Smooth and creamy, this simple soup can be served warm as an appealing appetizer or light main course, but is also delicious cold, as vichyssoise. It is important that you wash leeks very carefully before using them, as any grit that is not washed off can ruin a dish.

SERVES 4–6

25g/1oz/2 tbsp unsalted butter

1 onion, thinly sliced

2–3 leeks (white and pale green parts only), thinly sliced and well rinsed

3 garlic cloves, roughly chopped

120ml/4fl oz/1/2 cup dry white vermouth or white wine (optional)

3 medium waxy potatoes, peeled and chopped small

1.5 litres/21/2 pints/61/4 cups vegetable stock

3 sprigs fresh parsley

3 sprigs fresh thyme

1 bay leaf

200ml/7fl oz/scant 1 cup single (light) cream or milk (optional)

salt and ground white pepper

30ml/2 tbsp thinly chopped fresh chives or chopped parsley, to garnish

1 Heat the butter in a large pan over a medium heat. Add the onion, leeks and garlic to the pan and sauté for 12 minutes, stirring occasionally, until softened but not browned.

2 Increase the heat to high and pour in the vermouth or wine, if using. Boil vigorously for about 4 minutes, or until the mixture is almost dry. Add the potatoes and stock.

3 Tie the fresh parsley, thyme and bay leaf together with a piece of kitchen string (twine). Add this to the soup.

4 Bring to the boil, lower the heat and cover the pan, leaving the lid slightly ajar to let the excess steam escape. Simmer for 20 minutes, until tender.

5 Lift out and discard the tied herbs. With a hand-held blender or in a food processor, purée the soup until the desired consistency is reached.

6 If using the milk or cream, whisk it into the soup. Season and heat through. Divide among warm soup bowls, garnish with chives or parsley and serve immediately.

Nutritional information per portion: Energy 127kcal/534kJ; Protein 3.4g; Carbohydrate 19.6g, of which sugars 3.9g; Fat 4.4g, of which saturates 2.4g; Cholesterol 9mg; Calcium 40mg; Fibre 3.2g; Sodium 180mg.

Chicory soup

This velvety soup is both light and elegant, and makes the perfect appetizer for a sophisticated winter supper. It is also delicious when served chilled in ice-cold shot glasses for a delicate amuse-bouche, which is served before the hors d'oeuvre or first course of a meal.

SERVES 4

25g/1oz/2 tbsp unsalted butter
1 white onion, chopped
3 garlic cloves, chopped
8 chicory (Belgian endive), cored
   and chopped
2 medium potatoes, peeled and chopped
1 litre/1³/₄ pints/4 cups vegetable stock
500ml/17fl oz/generous 2 cups single
   (light) cream or milk
pinch of nutmeg
salt and white pepper
4 small chicory leaves, 4 dill sprigs
   and 4 chive blades, to garnish

1 Melt the butter in a medium pan and sauté the chopped onion over a medium heat for 5 minutes until it has softened but not browned.

2 Add the garlic and chopped chicory and sauté for 5 minutes more. Add the potatoes and stock, bring to the boil, reduce the heat and simmer for about 30 minutes or until the potatoes are soft.

3 Pour in the cream and heat through. With a hand-held blender or in a food processor, blend until the desired consistency is reached.

4 Add nutmeg, salt and white pepper to taste, and reheat the soup.

5 Ladle the soup into bowls and garnish with the dill, chives and small chicory leaves.

Nutritional information per portion: Energy 185kcal/778kJ; Protein 6.4g; Carbohydrate 24.6g, of which sugars 8.4g; Fat 7.9g, of which saturates 4.8g; Cholesterol 21mg; Calcium 172mg; Fibre 1.7g; Sodium 104mg.

Borscht

Most people think that borscht is a Russian dish, but in fact the original borscht comes from the Ukraine. This vegetarian version, which contains red cabbage, carrot and apple as well as beetroot, is delicately flavoured with caraway seeds and bay.

SERVES 6–8

20g/³⁄₄oz/1¹⁄₂ tbsp butter

15ml/1 tbsp caraway seeds

800g/1³⁄₄lb beetroot (beets), grated

1 small red cabbage, finely shredded

1 large cooking apple, grated

30ml/2 tbsp vinegar (any kind)

2 carrots, grated

1 bay leaf

2 garlic cloves

2 litres/3¹⁄₂ pints/8³⁄₄ cups vegetable stock

salt and ground black pepper

3 hard-boiled eggs, chopped, to garnish

100ml/3¹⁄₂fl oz/scant ¹⁄₂ cup sour
   cream, to serve

1 Heat the butter in a large, heavy pan over a medium heat. When melted, add the caraway seeds and beetroot, and stir to coat in the butter. Season to taste.

2 Add the cabbage and apple to the pan, then the vinegar, carrots, bay leaf and garlic, and pour in the stock.

3 Cover the pan and leave to simmer over a gentle heat for 2 hours, adding a little water if the liquid reduces too much.

4 Serve the hot borscht topped with a scattering of the chopped hard-boiled egg, and hand the sour cream round separately.

Nutritional information per portion: Energy 109kcal/456kJ; Protein 5g; Carbohydrate 13.2g, of which sugars 12.4g; Fat 4.4g, of which saturates 2g; Cholesterol 77mg; Calcium 62mg; Fibre 3.8g; Sodium 121mg.

Wild mushroom soup

This creamy soup is really special when made with fresh wild mushrooms, although a combination of button and dried mushrooms can be used if they are unavailable. If you are planning on foraging for your own mushrooms, then always consult an expert before cooking them, to ensure they are edible.

SERVES 4

400g/14oz mushrooms, preferably
    wild, sliced, or, if using button (white)
    mushrooms, use an additional
    10g/¼oz/1 tbsp dried mushrooms,
    such as ceps
1.25 litres/2¼ pints/5½ cups light
    vegetable stock
50g/2oz/4 tbsp butter

30–45ml/2–3 tbsp plain (all-purpose)
    white flour
60ml/4 tbsp double (heavy) cream, plus
    extra to serve
a squeeze of fresh lemon juice
15–30ml/1–2 tbsp medium sherry (optional)
salt and ground black pepper
chopped fresh parsley, to garnish

1 If using dried mushrooms, put in a small bowl and pour over a generous amount of boiling water. Leave to soak for at least 20 minutes, until the mushrooms are soft. Using a slotted spoon, remove the mushrooms from the bowl then strain the soaking liquid and reserve. Chop the soaked mushrooms.

2 Put the sliced fresh mushrooms in a pan, cover with the stock and simmer for 10 minutes. Strain the stock and reserve.

3 Melt the butter in a large pan, add the sliced mushrooms and the soaked mushrooms, if using, and fry gently for 2–3 minutes, then season with salt and pepper.

4 Stir the flour into the pan and cook over a low heat for 1–2 minutes, without colouring. Remove from the heat and gradually stir in the reserved stock and the dried mushroom soaking liquid, if using, to form a smooth sauce. Return to the heat and, stirring constantly, cook until the sauce boils and thickens. Lower the heat and simmer gently for 5–10 minutes.

5 Add the cream to the soup then add lemon juice to taste. Finally, add the sherry, if using. Pour the soup into individual serving bowls, with a little cream swirled on top of each. Garnish with the chopped parsley, and serve.

Nutritional information per portion: Energy 154kcal/638kJ; Protein 3.2g; Carbohydrate 9.3g, of which sugars 0.5g; Fat 11.8g, of which saturates 7.2g; Cholesterol 29mg; Calcium 26mg; Fibre 1.6g; Sodium 82mg.

Cold barley and mushroom soup

Barley and mushrooms form the basis of this hearty soup, which is packed full of distinctive flavours and has the unmistakable tang of lemon juice and sour cream. This soup is served cold, garnished with chopped eggs and feathery dill, and makes an excellent alfresco lunch in summer.

SERVES 6

150g/5oz/generous ¹/₂ cup pearl barley

45ml/3 tbsp vegetable oil

1 onion, thinly sliced

400g/14oz/5¹/₂ cups mushrooms,
    thinly sliced

45ml/3 tbsp lemon juice

1 litre/1³/₄ pints/4 cups vegetable stock

200ml/7fl oz/scant 1 cup sour cream

45ml/3 tbsp dill, finely chopped

salt and ground black pepper

2 hard-boiled eggs, finely chopped,
    to garnish

1 Put the barley in a large bowl and cover with cold water. Soak overnight in a cool place, then drain. Heat the oil in a large, heavy pan and cook the onions for 5 minutes, or until softened but not browned.

2 Add the mushrooms and cook for a further 10 minutes. Add the lemon juice and barley, and stir well.

3 Pour in the stock, then bring to the boil. Simmer for 45 minutes, or until the barley is cooked and soft. Season to taste, then leave to cool.

4 Stir in the sour cream and dill, reserving a little dill to garnish. Chill the soup, then ladle the cold soup into bowls and serve, garnished with the chopped eggs and dill.

Nutritional information per portion: Energy 247kcal/1033kJ; Protein 6.6g; Carbohydrate 23.4g, of which sugars 2.1g; Fat 14.9g, of which saturates 5.3g; Cholesterol 83mg; Calcium 67mg; Fibre 1.3g; Sodium 44mg.

Butter bean soup

Beans are rich in carbohydrate, protein and fibre, so are perfect for the vegetarian diet. They are also ideal for adding bulk, flavour and texture to soups and stews. Here butter beans form the basis of a delicately-spiced and substantial soup that makes a comforting supper.

SERVES 6

250g/9oz/1¼ cups butter (lima) beans, soaked overnight in plenty of water

2 large white potatoes, peeled and quartered

2 vegetable stock (bouillon) cubes

75ml/5 tbsp vegetable oil

1 medium red onion, finely chopped

1 garlic clove, finely chopped

2.5ml/½ tsp paprika

2.5ml/½ tsp dried oregano

250ml/8fl oz/1 cup full cream (whole) milk

45ml/3 tbsp hard, strong cheese, such as Parmesan, grated, to serve

salt

1 Wash and drain the butter beans and put them in a large pan with 2 litres/3½ pints/8 cups fresh water. Bring the beans to the boil, cover and simmer over a gentle heat for 1 hour, until tender.

2 Meanwhile, put the potatoes in a large pan with 1 litre/1¾ pints/4 cups water and the stock cubes. Bring to the boil, cover and simmer for 15 minutes, until tender. Remove from the heat and set aside.

3 Heat the oil in a frying pan over a medium heat and fry the onion with the garlic for 10 minutes, adding the paprika and oregano when they begin to caramelize. Add this mixture to the pan of potatoes and stock, then add the beans and their cooking water.

4 Bring the soup to the boil, reduce the heat and simmer for 5 minutes. Add the milk, season to taste and serve with grated cheese.

Nutritional information per portion: Energy 305kcal/1280kJ; Protein 14.9g; Carbohydrate 31.9g, of which sugars 4.5g; Fat 14.1g, of which saturates 3.7g; Cholesterol 13mg; Calcium 187mg; Fibre 7.4g; Sodium 241mg.

Cannellini bean soup

This traditional Greek dish is usually served with bread and olives, and perhaps raw onion quarters (or raw garlic for those with robust palates). The hearty combination of carrots, cannellini beans and tomatoes makes this soup a rewarding and substantial lunch.

SERVES 4

275g/10oz/1½ cups dried cannellini
   beans, soaked overnight in cold water
1 large onion, thinly sliced
1 celery stick, sliced
2–3 carrots, sliced in discs
400g/14oz can tomatoes
15ml/1 tbsp tomato purée (paste)
150ml/¼ pint/⅔ cup extra virgin
   olive oil
5ml/1 tsp dried oregano
30ml/2 tbsp finely chopped fresh flat
   leaf parsley
salt and ground black pepper

1 Drain the beans, rinse them under cold water and drain them again. Transfer them to a large pan, pour in enough water to cover and bring to the boil. Cook for about 3 minutes, then drain.

2 Return the beans to the pan, pour in fresh water to cover them by about 3cm/1¼in, then add the onion, celery, carrots and tomatoes, and stir in the tomato purée, olive oil and oregano. Season with a little pepper, but don't add salt at this stage, as it will toughen the skins of the beans.

3 Bring to the boil, lower the heat and cook for about 1 hour, until the beans are just tender. Season with salt, stir in the parsley and serve.

Nutritional information per portion: Energy 460Kcal/1922kJ; Protein 16.8g; Carbohydrate 41.1g, of which sugars 11.8g; Fat 26.5g, of which saturates 3.9g; Cholesterol 0mg; Calcium 103mg; Fibre 14g; Sodium 54mg.

Chestnut and white bean soup

Chesnuts are an essential ingredient for the vegetarian store cupboard. They can be bought dried or frozen, but are at their best when freshly harvested on a chilly winter walk. This delicious soup combines sweet chestnuts with protein-packed haricot beans for a hearty winter warmer.

SERVES 4

100g/3³/4oz/¹/₂ cup dried haricot beans,
**   soaked overnight in cold water**
**   and drained**
90g/3¹/₂oz peeled chestnuts, thawed
**   if frozen**
1 bay leaf
50ml/2fl oz/¹/₄ cup olive oil
1 onion, chopped
salt

1 Put the beans, chestnuts and bay leaf in a pan, pour in 1 litre/1³/4 pints/ 4 cups of water and bring to the boil. Lower the heat and cook for about 1¹/₂ hours, until tender.

2 Meanwhile, heat the oil in a frying pan. Add the onion and cook over a low heat, stirring occasionally, for 5 minutes, until softened. Add it to the soup. Season to taste with salt, remove and discard the bay leaf and mash the beans and chestnuts with a fork. Serve immediately.

Nutritional information per portion: Energy 184kcal/773kJ; Protein 6.2g; Carbohydrate 20.5g, of which sugars 3.1g; Fat 9.2g, of which saturates 1.4g; Cholesterol 0mg; Calcium 39mg; Fibre 5.1g; Sodium 8mg.

Lentil soup

Lentils make an easy option for a quick meal, as they do not need soaking. This soup is packed with the flavours of the Mediterranean, and the key to its success is to be generous with the olive oil. Serve as a main meal, accompanied by olives, bread and cheese.

SERVES 4

275g/10oz/1¼ cups brown-green lentils, preferably a small variety
150ml/¼ pint/⅔ cup extra virgin olive oil
1 onion, thinly sliced
2 garlic cloves, sliced into thin batons
1 carrot, sliced into thin discs
400g/14oz can chopped tomatoes
15ml/1 tbsp tomato purée (paste)
2.5ml/½ tsp dried oregano
1 litre/1¾ pints/4 cups hot water
salt and ground black pepper
30ml/2 tbsp roughly chopped fresh herb leaves, to garnish

1 Rinse the lentils, drain them and put them in a large pan with cold water to cover. Bring to the boil and boil for 3–4 minutes. Strain, discarding the liquid, and set the lentils aside.

2 Wipe the pan clean, heat the olive oil in it, then add the onion and sauté until translucent. Stir in the garlic, then, as soon as it becomes aromatic, return the lentils to the pan.

3 Add the carrot, tomatoes, tomato purée and oregano to the pan. Stir in the hot water and a little ground black pepper to taste.

4 Bring the soup to the boil, then lower the heat, cover the pan and cook over a gentle heat for 20–30 minutes until the lentils feel soft but have not yet begun to disintegrate. Add salt and the chopped herbs just before serving.

Nutritional information per portion: Energy 463Kcal/1937kJ; Protein 17.9g; Carbohydrate 40.4g, of which sugars 7.2g; Fat 26.7g, of which saturates 3.9g; Cholesterol 0mg; Calcium 67mg; Fibre 8g; Sodium 33mg.

Spicy red lentil soup with onion and parsley

This lentil soup is light and subtly spiced, and delicious when served as an appetizer or snack. The aromatic flavours of chilli, cumin, coriander and fenugreek combine to make it beautifully fragrant, with just a trace of underlying heat. It is a real treat for the senses.

SERVES 4–6

30–45ml/2–3 tbsp olive or sunflower oil

1 large onion, finely chopped

2 garlic cloves, finely chopped

1 fresh red chilli, seeded and finely chopped

5–10ml/1–2 tsp cumin seeds

5–10ml/1–2 tsp coriander seeds

1 carrot, finely chopped

scant 5ml/1 tsp ground fenugreek

5ml/1 tsp sugar

15ml/1 tbsp tomato purée (paste)

250g/9oz/generous 1 cup split red lentils

1.75 litres/3 pints/7½ cups vegetable stock

salt and ground black pepper

1 small red onion, finely chopped,
   to garnish

1 bunch of fresh flat leaf parsley,
   chopped, to garnish

4–6 lemon wedges, to serve

1 Heat the oil in a heavy pan and stir in the onion, garlic, chilli, cumin and coriander seeds. When the onion begins to colour, toss in the carrot and cook for 2–3 minutes. Add the fenugreek, sugar and tomato purée and stir in the lentils.

2 Pour in the stock, stir well and bring to the boil. Lower the heat, partially cover the pan and simmer for 30–40 minutes, until the lentils have broken up.

3 If the soup is too thick, thin it down with a little water. Season the soup with salt and ground black pepper to taste.

4 Serve the soup straight from the pan or, if you prefer a smooth texture, purée it in a blender, then reheat if necessary. Ladle the soup into bowls and sprinkle liberally with the chopped onion and parsley. Serve with a wedge of lemon to squeeze over the soup.

Nutritional information per portion: Energy 203kcal/856kJ; Protein 11.1g; Carbohydrate 31.8g, of which sugars 7.3g; Fat 4.4g, of which saturates 0.6g; Cholesterol 0mg; Calcium 45mg; Fibre 3.5g; Sodium 26mg.

Cinnamon-scented chickpea and lentil soup with fennel and honey buns

This thick pulse and vegetable soup, flavoured with ginger and cinnamon, is served with fragrant honey-flavoured buns, making it a substantial meal in its own right.

SERVES 8

30–45ml/2–3 tbsp olive oil
2 onions, halved and sliced
2.5ml/¹⁄₂ tsp ground ginger
2.5ml/¹⁄₂ tsp ground turmeric
5ml/1 tsp ground cinnamon
pinch of saffron threads
2 x 400g/14oz cans chopped tomatoes
5–10ml/1–2 tsp caster (superfine) sugar
175g/6oz/³⁄₄ cup brown or green lentils,
    picked over and rinsed
about 1.75 litres/3 pints/7¹⁄₂ cups vegetable
    stock, or water
200g/7oz/1 generous cup dried broad (fava)
    beans, soaked overnight and boiled
    until tender

200g/7oz/1 generous cup dried chickpeas,
    soaked overnight and boiled until tender
small bunch of fresh coriander
    (cilantro), chopped
small bunch of flat leaf parsley, chopped
salt and ground black pepper

FOR THE HONEY BUNS

2.5ml/¹⁄₂ tsp dried yeast
300g/11oz/1¹⁄₄ cups unbleached strong
    white bread flour
15–30ml/1–2 tbsp clear honey
5ml/1 tsp fennel seeds
250ml/8fl oz/1 cup milk
1 egg yolk, stirred with a little milk
salt

1 Make the honey buns. Dissolve the yeast in about 15ml/1 tbsp lukewarm water. Sift the flour and a pinch of salt into a bowl. Make a well in the centre and add the dissolved yeast, honey and fennel seeds. Gradually pour in the milk, using your hands to work it into the flour along with the honey, fennel seeds and yeast, until the mixture forms a dough. (If the dough becomes too sticky to handle, add more flour.)

2 Turn the dough out on to a floured surface and knead well for about 10 minutes, until it is smooth and elastic. Flour the surface under the dough and cover it with a damp cloth, then leave the dough to rise until it has doubled in size. This should take around 1 hour.

3 Preheat the oven to 230°C/450°F/Gas 8. Grease two baking sheets. Divide the dough into 12 balls. On a floured surface, flatten the balls of dough with the palm of your hand, then place them on a baking sheet. Brush the tops of the buns with egg yolk, then bake for about 15 minutes until they are risen slightly and sound hollow when tapped underneath. Transfer to a wire rack to cool.

4 To make the soup, heat the olive oil in a stockpot or large pan. Add the onions and stir for about 15 minutes, or until they are soft.

5 Add the ginger, turmeric, cinnamon and saffron, followed by the tomatoes and a little of the sugar. Stir in the lentils and pour in the stock or water. Bring the liquid to the boil, then reduce the heat, cover and simmer for about 25 minutes, or until the lentils are tender.

6 Stir in the cooked beans and chickpeas, bring back to the boil, then cover and simmer for a further 10–15 minutes. Stir in the fresh herbs and season the soup to taste. Serve piping hot, with the honey buns.

Nutritional information per portion: Energy 368Kcal/1558kJ; Protein 18.3g; Carbohydrate 64.9g, of which sugars 9.7g; Fat 5.7g, of which saturates 1g; Cholesterol 2mg; Calcium 172mg; Fibre 7.5g; Sodium 74mg.

Velvety pumpkin soup with rice and cinnamon

This fragrant pumpkin and cinnamon soup is simple to make and packed with flavour. Adding rice to the soup makes this a real feast, but this can be omitted if you are looking for a lighter meal.

SERVES 4

about 1.1kg/2lb 7oz pumpkin
750ml/1¼ pints/3 cups vegetable stock
750ml/1¼ pints/3 cups milk
10–15ml/2–3 tsp sugar
75g/3oz/½ cup cooked white rice
salt and ground black pepper
5ml/1 tsp ground cinnamon, to serve

1 Remove any seeds or fibre from the pumpkin, cut off the peel and chop the flesh. Put the prepared pumpkin in a pan and add the stock, milk, sugar and seasoning.

2 Bring the pan to the boil, then reduce the heat and simmer for about 20 minutes, or until the pumpkin is tender.

3 Drain the pumpkin, reserving the liquid, and purée it in a food processor, then return it to the pan.

4 Bring the soup back to the boil again, add the rice and simmer for a few minutes, until the grains are reheated. Check the seasoning, dust with cinnamon and pour into bowls. Serve piping hot, with chunks of bread.

Nutritional information per portion: Energy 202Kcal/856kJ; Protein 9.7g; Carbohydrate 33.1g, of which sugars 15.6g; Fat 4.4g, of which saturates 2.5g; Cholesterol 11mg; Calcium 315mg; Fibre 2.8g; Sodium 82mg.

Chunky tomato soup with noodles

This full-flavoured Moroccan soup has a lovely, warming kick. It is especially delicious when finished with a swirl of yogurt and finely chopped coriander, and served with chunks of fresh bread.

SERVES 4

45–60ml/3–4 tbsp olive oil

3–4 cloves

2 onions, chopped

1 butternut squash, peeled, seeded and
   cut into small chunks

4 celery stalks, chopped

2 carrots, peeled and chopped

8 large tomatoes, skinned and chopped

5–10ml/1–2 tsp sugar

15ml/1 tbsp tomato purée (paste)

5–10ml/1–2 tsp ras el hanout

2.5ml/¹⁄₂ tsp ground turmeric

a big bunch of fresh coriander (cilantro),
   chopped, plus extra to garnish

1.75 litres/3 pints/7¹⁄₂ cups vegetable stock

a handful dried egg noodles, broken
   into pieces

salt and ground black pepper

60–75ml/4–5 tbsp creamy yogurt, to serve

1 In a deep, heavy pan, heat the oil and add the cloves, onions, squash, celery and carrots. Fry until they begin to colour, then stir in the tomatoes and sugar. Cook the tomatoes until the water reduces and they begin to pulp.

2 Stir in the tomato purée, ras el hanout, turmeric and chopped coriander. Pour in the stock and bring the liquid to the boil. Reduce the heat and simmer for 30–40 minutes until the vegetables are very tender and the liquid has reduced a little.

3 To make a puréed soup, leave the liquid to cool slightly before processing in a food processor or blender, then pour back into the pan and add the noodles. Alternatively, to make a chunky soup, simply add the noodles to the unblended soup and cook for a further 8–10 minutes, or until the noodles are soft.

4 Season the soup to taste and ladle it into bowls. Swirl a spoonful of yogurt into each one, garnish with coriander and serve with chunks of fresh bread.

Nutritional information per portion: Energy 265Kcal/1108kJ; Protein 6.9g; Carbohydrate 37.8g, of which sugars 20.2g; Fat 10.2g, of which saturates 1.7g; Cholesterol 0mg; Calcium 158mg; Fibre 8.1g; Sodium 64mg.

Curry soup

This aromatic soup is subtly flavoured with Indian spices and thickened with creamy coconut milk. The chopped apple adds a delicious underlying sweetness that complements the curry spices and makes this the ideal appetizer for a vegetarian Indian meal.

SERVES 4

50g/2oz/4 tbsp butter

2 shallots, finely chopped

1 cooking apple, peeled, cored
   and chopped

10ml/2 tsp curry paste

30ml/2 tbsp plain (all-purpose) flour

1.25 litres/2¼ pints/5½ cups
   vegetable stock

400ml/14fl oz can unsweetened
   coconut milk

salt and ground black pepper

chopped fresh parsley, to garnish

60ml/4 tbsp double (heavy) cream or
   4 tbsp of the coconut milk, to serve

1 Melt the butter in a pan, add the shallots and cook gently for about 5 minutes until softened but not coloured. Add the apple, season with salt and pepper and cook for another 2 minutes, until the apple is slightly softened.

2 Stir the curry paste and flour into the pan and cook over a low heat for 1–2 minutes, without colouring. Remove from the heat and gradually stir in the stock to form a smooth sauce.

3 Return to the heat and, stirring constantly, cook until the sauce boils and thickens. Lower the heat to a gentle simmer and allow to cook for a further 10 minutes.

4 Add the coconut milk to the soup and stir well. Check the seasonings, adding salt and pepper if necessary. Pour the soup into individual serving bowls and serve with a swirl of cream or coconut milk on top of each and chopped parsley, to garnish.

Nutritional information per portion: Energy 195kcal/812kJ; Protein 1.7g; Carbohydrate 14.3g, of which sugars 7.6g; Fat 15g, of which saturates 9.2g; Cholesterol 37mg; Calcium 66mg; Fibre 1.3g; Sodium 200mg.

Pumpkin, snake bean and bamboo soup with coconut

This tasty Indonesian soup is served with rice and, when packed with vegetables, makes an extremely satisfying vegetarian meal. This dish can be accompanied by a chilli sambal, which can be made by pounding chillies with lime juice, or with ginger and garlic.

SERVES FOUR

30ml/2 tbsp palm, groundnut (peanut) oil
150g/5oz pumpkin flesh
115g/4oz snake (yard-long) beans, chopped
220g/7½oz can bamboo shoots
900ml/1½ pints coconut milk
10–15ml/2–3 tsp palm sugar (jaggery)
130g/4½oz fresh coconut, shredded
salt

FOR THE SPICE PASTE

4 shallots, chopped
25g/1oz fresh root ginger, chopped
4 red chillies, seeded and chopped
2 garlic cloves, chopped
5ml/1 tsp coriander seeds
4 candlenuts, toasted and chopped

TO SERVE
cooked rice
chilli sambal

1 To make the spice paste, using a mortar and pestle, grind all the ingredients together to form a smooth paste, or blend them together in an electric blender or food processor.

2 Heat the oil in a wok or large, heavy pan, stir in the spice paste and fry until fragrant. Toss the pumpkin, snake beans and bamboo shoots in the paste.

3 Pour in the coconut milk. Add the sugar and bring to the boil. Reduce the heat and cook for 5–10 minutes, until the vegetables are tender.

4 Season the soup with salt to taste and stir in half the fresh coconut. Ladle the soup into individual warmed bowls, sprinkle with the remaining coconut and serve with bowls of cooked rice to spoon over the soup and a chilli sambal.

Nutritional information per portion: Energy 333kcal/1388kJ; Protein 6g; Carbohydrate 26g, of which sugars 23.8g; Fat 23.6g, of which saturates 11.7g; Cholesterol 0mg; Calcium 115mg; Fibre 4.9g; Sodium 258mg.

Appetizers

The perfect appetizer can set the tone of a meal, and heighten your guest's expectations about what is to come. This chapter features delicious vegetarian first courses to suit every occasion, from simple and elegant dishes like Walnut and Goat's Cheese Bruschetta, or Tomato and Tapenade Tarts, through to impressive and unusual offerings, such as Turkish Stuffed Aubergines, or Beansprout and Cucumber Parcels.

Red onion and mushroom tartlets with goat's cheese

Crisp and savoury, these little tarts combine sweet caramelized onions with earthy goat's cheese. Especially delicious when served with mixed salad leaves drizzled with a garlic-infused dressing.

SERVES 6

60ml/4 tbsp olive oil
25g/1oz/2 tbsp butter
4 red onions, thinly sliced
5ml/1 tsp brown sugar
15ml/1 tbsp balsamic vinegar
15ml/1 tbsp soy sauce
200g/7oz button (white) mushrooms, sliced
1 garlic clove, finely chopped
2.5ml/^{1}/$_2$ tsp chopped fresh tarragon
30ml/2 tbsp chopped fresh parsley

250g/9oz goat's cheese log (chèvre)
salt and ground black pepper
mixed salad leaves, to serve

FOR THE PASTRY

200g/7oz/1^3/$_4$ cups plain (all-purpose) flour
pinch of cayenne pepper
90g/3^1/$_2$oz/7 tbsp butter
40g/1^1/$_2$oz/^{1}/$_2$ cup grated Parmesan cheese
45–60ml/3–4 tbsp iced water

1 First make the pastry. Sift the flour and cayenne into a bowl, add the butter, then rub in with the fingertips until the mixture resembles breadcrumbs.

2 Stir in the grated Parmesan, then bind the pastry with the iced water, adding just enough to give a firm dough. Press the pastry together into a ball, then wrap it in clear film (plastic wrap) and chill for at least 45 minutes.

3 Heat 15ml/1 tbsp of the oil and half the butter in a heavy frying pan, then add the onions, cover and cook gently for 15 minutes, stirring occasionally.

4 Uncover the pan, increase the heat slightly and sprinkle in the brown sugar. Cook, stirring frequently, until the onions begin to caramelize and brown. Add the vinegar and soy sauce, and cook briskly until the liquid evaporates. Season to taste then set aside.

5 Heat another 30ml/2 tbsp of the oil and the remaining butter in a pan, then add the mushrooms and garlic, and cook fairly briskly for 5–6 minutes, until the mushrooms are browned and cooked.

6 Set a few mushrooms and onion rings aside, then stir the rest of the mushrooms into the onions with the tarragon and parsley. Adjust the seasoning to taste. Preheat the oven to 190°C/375°F/Gas 5.

7 Roll out the pastry and use to line 6 x 10cm/4in tartlet tins (muffin pans), preferably loose-based and metal. Prick the pastry bases with a fork and line the sides with strips of foil. Bake for 10 minutes, remove the foil and bake for another 5–7 minutes, or until the pastry is lightly browned and cooked. Remove from the oven and increase the temperature to 200°C/400°F/Gas 6.

8 Remove the pastry shells from the tins and place on a baking sheet. Divide the onion mixture among the pastry shells. Cut the goat's cheese into 6 slices and place 1 slice on each tartlet. Add a few reserved mushrooms and onion slices to each tartlet, drizzle with the remaining oil and season with pepper.

9 Return the tartlets to the oven and bake for 5–8 minutes, or until the goat's cheese is just beginning to turn brown. Serve with mixed salad leaves.

Nutritional information per portion: Energy 595Kcal/2482kJ; Protein 15.4g; Carbohydrate 50.8g, of which sugars 8.1g; Fat 39.4g, of which saturates 5.9g; Cholesterol 74mg; Calcium 139mg; Fibre 1.6g; Sodium 543mg.

Red onion and olive pissaladière

For a taste of the Mediterranean, try this tasty French-style pizza topped with sweet red onion.
It makes a delicious and easy snack and is perfect for lazy summer days.

SERVES 6

75ml/5 tbsp extra virgin olive oil,
   plus extra for drizzling (optional)
500g/1¼ lb small red onions, thinly
   sliced
500g/1¼ lb puff pastry, thawed if frozen
plain (all-purpose) flour, for dusting
75g/3oz/¾ cup small pitted black olives
salt and ground black pepper

1 Preheat the oven to 220°C/
425°F/Gas 7. Heat the oil in a large,
heavy frying pan and cook the
onions gently, stirring frequently, for
15–20 minutes, until they are soft
and golden. Season to taste.

2 Roll out the pastry thinly on a
floured surface. Cut out a 33cm/13in
round and place on a baking sheet.

3 Spread the onions over the pastry
in an even layer to within 1cm/½ in
of the edge.

4 Sprinkle the olives over the
pissaladière. Bake for 20–25 minutes,
until the pastry is risen and golden
in colour. Cut into wedges, drizzle
with olive oil, if required, and
serve warm.

Nutritional information per portion: Energy 436Kcal/1815kJ; Protein 5.9g; Carbohydrate 37.4g, of which sugars 5.8g;
Fat 31.1g, of which saturates 1.5g; Cholesterol 0mg; Calcium 77mg; Fibre 1.5g; Sodium 542mg.

Tomato and tapenade tarts

These tempting individual tarts look and taste fantastic, and demand very little time or effort.
The mascarpone cheese topping melts as it cooks to make a smooth, creamy sauce.

SERVES 4

oil, for greasing
500g/1¼ lb puff pastry, thawed if frozen
plain (all-purpose) flour, for dusting
60ml/4 tbsp green olive tapenade
500g/1¼ lb cherry tomatoes
90g/3½oz/scant ½ cup mascarpone
   cheese
salt and ground black peper

1 Preheat the oven to 220°C/ 425°F/Gas 7. Lightly grease a large baking sheet and sprinkle it with water. Roll out the pastry on a lightly floured surface and cut out four 16cm/6½in rounds, using a bowl or small plate as a guide.

2 Transfer the pastry rounds to the prepared baking sheet. Using the tip of a sharp knife, mark a shallow cut 1cm/½in in from the edge of each round to form a rim.

3 Spread half the tapenade over the pastry rounds, keeping it inside the marked rim. Cut half the tomatoes in half. Pile all of the tomatoes on the pastry, keeping them inside the rim. Season lightly.

4 Bake for 20 minutes. Dot with the remaining tapenade. Spoon a little mascarpone on the centre of the tomatoes and season. Bake for a further 10 minutes, until the mascarpone has melted. Serve warm.

Nutritional information per portion: Energy 543Kcal/2269kJ; Protein 10.2g; Carbohydrate 50.8g, of which sugars 6.2g; Fat 35.9g, of which saturates 2.4g; Cholesterol 9mg; Calcium 91mg; Fibre 1.7g; Sodium 736mg.

Stilton-stuffed mushrooms baked in breadcrumbs

These succulent Stilton-stuffed mushrooms are especially delicious when served with chunks of warm, crusty bread or fresh rolls to soak up all their irresistible garlic-flavoured juices.

SERVES 4

450g/1lb chestnut mushrooms
3 garlic cloves, finely chopped
90g/3½oz/7 tbsp butter, melted
juice of ½ lemon
115g/4oz Stilton cheese, crumbled
50g/2oz/½ cup walnuts, chopped
90g/3½oz/1½ cups fresh white
    breadcrumbs
25g/1oz Parmesan cheese, grated
30ml/2 tbsp chopped fresh parsley
salt and ground black pepper

1 Preheat the oven to 200°C/400°F /Gas 6. Place the chestnut mushrooms in an ovenproof dish and sprinkle half the garlic over them. Drizzle with 50g/2oz/4 tbsp of the melted butter and the lemon juice. Season with salt and pepper and bake for 15–20 minutes. Leave to cool.

2 Cream the crumbled Stilton with the chopped walnuts and mix in 25g/1oz/2 tbsp of the breadcrumbs.

3 Divide the Stilton mixture among the mushrooms.

4 Preheat the grill (broiler). Mix the remaining garlic, breadcrumbs and melted butter together. Stir in the Parmesan and parsley and season with pepper.

5 Cover the mushrooms with the breadcrumb mixture and grill (broil) for about 5 minutes, or until crisp and browned. Serve immediately.

Nutritional information per portion: Energy 416kcal/1719kJ; Protein 13.3g; Carbohydrate 1.2g, of which sugars 0.8g; Fat 39.5g, of which saturates 20.6g; Cholesterol 88mg; Calcium 209mg; Fibre 2.2g; Sodium 514mg.

Baked eggs en cocotte with wild mushrooms

These simple, but utterly delectable, baked eggs make a splendid start to a light meal or an excellent dish for brunch. Serve with hot, buttered wholemeal toast.

SERVES 4–6

65g/2¹/₂oz/5 tbsp butter
2 shallots, finely chopped
1 small garlic clove, finely chopped
250g/9oz mixed mushrooms,
   finely chopped
15ml/1 tbsp lemon juice
5ml/1 tsp chopped fresh tarragon
30ml/2 tbsp crème fraîche
30ml/2 tbsp chopped fresh chives
4–6 eggs
salt and ground black pepper
whole chives, to garnish
buttered wholemeal (whole-wheat)
   toast, to serve

1 Melt 50g/2oz/4 tbsp of the butter in a pan over a low heat and cook the shallots and garlic gently, stirring occasionally, for 5 minutes, until softened but not browned.

2 Increase the heat and add the mushrooms, then cook, stirring frequently, until the mushrooms lose their moisture and begin to brown.

3 Stir in the lemon juice and tarragon and cook over a medium heat, stirring occasionally, until the mushrooms absorb the liquid. Stir in half the crème fraîche and half the chopped chives, and season to taste.

4 Preheat the oven to 190°C/ 375°F/Gas 5. Divide the mushroom mixture equally among 4–6 large ramekins of about 150–175ml/ 5–6fl oz/²/₃–³/₄ cup capacity. Sprinkle over the remaining chives.

5 Break an egg into each dish, add a dab of crème fraîche and season to taste with black pepper. Dot with the remaining butter and bake for 10–15 minutes, until the whites of the eggs are set and the yolks cooked to your liking.

6 Serve immediately, accompanied by hot, buttered wholemeal toast.

Nutritional information per portion: Energy 169kcal/700kJ; Protein 6.3g; Carbohydrate 1.1g, of which sugars 0.8g; Fat 15.7g, of which saturates 8.5g; Cholesterol 189mg; Calcium 35mg; Fibre 0.6g; Sodium 143mg.

Mushroom and bean pâté

This light and tasty pâté is cooked in a slow cooker, and is especially good when served on wholemeal toast. It makes an ideal vegetarian appetizer or light lunch served with salad.

SERVES 8

450g/1lb/6 cups mushrooms, sliced

1 onion, finely chopped

2 garlic cloves, crushed

1 red (bell) pepper, seeded and diced

30ml/2 tbsp vegetable stock

30ml/2 tbsp dry white wine

400g/14oz can red kidney beans, rinsed
   and drained

oil, for greasing

1 egg, beaten

50g/2oz/1 cup fresh wholemeal (whole-
   wheat) breadcrumbs

10ml/2 tsp chopped fresh thyme

10ml/2 tsp chopped fresh rosemary

salt and ground black pepper

wholemeal (whole-wheat) toast, salad
   leaves, fresh herbs and tomato
   wedges, to serve

1 Put the mushrooms, onion, garlic, red pepper, vegetable stock and wine in a slow cooker. Cover and cook on high for 2 hours, then set aside to cool.

2 Transfer the vegetables into a food processor or blender, and add the rinsed kidney beans. Process until smooth, stopping the machine once or twice to scrape down the sides.

3 Grease and line a 900g/2lb loaf tin (pan). Put an inverted saucer into the slow cooker. Pour in 2.5cm/1in of water, and switch the slow cooker to high.

4 Transfer the blended mixture to a bowl. Add the egg, breadcrumbs and herbs, and season. Mix thoroughly, then spoon into the tin and cover with cling film (plastic wrap) or foil.

5 Put the tin in the slow cooker and pour in enough boiling water to come just over halfway up the sides of the tin. Cover with the lid and cook on high for 4 hours, until lightly set.

6 Remove from the slow cooker, leave to cool and refrigerate for several hours. Turn out of the tin, remove the lining paper and serve in slices with salad and wholemeal toast.

Nutritional information per portion: Energy 85Kcal/358kJ; Protein 5.5g; Carbohydrate 12.3g, of which sugars 3.8g; Fat 1.6g, of which saturates 0.4g; Cholesterol 28mg; Calcium 47mg; Fibre 3.7g; Sodium 187mg.

Roast garlic, goat's cheese, walnut and herb pâté

The combination of sweet roasted garlic and goat's cheese is classic. This is particularly good made with the new season's walnuts, which are available in the early autumn.

SERVES 4

4 large garlic bulbs
4 fresh rosemary sprigs
8 fresh thyme sprigs
60ml/4 tbsp olive oil
sea salt and ground black pepper

FOR THE PÂTÉ
200g/7oz soft goat's cheese
5ml/1 tsp finely chopped fresh thyme
15ml/1 tbsp chopped fresh parsley
50g/2oz shelled walnuts, chopped
15ml/1 tbsp walnut oil (optional)
fresh thyme sprigs, to garnish

TO SERVE
4–8 slices sourdough bread
shelled walnuts

1 Preheat the oven to 180°C/350°F/Gas 4. Strip the papery skin from the garlic bulbs. Place them in an ovenproof dish large enough to hold them snugly. Tuck in the rosemary and thyme, drizzle the oil over and season to taste.

2 Cover the garlic closely with foil and bake for 50–60 minutes, basting once. Leave to cool.

3 Preheat the grill (broiler). To make the pâté, cream the cheese with the thyme, parsley and walnuts. Beat in 15ml/1 tbsp of the oil from the garlic and season, then transfer to a bowl.

4 Brush the sourdough bread with the remaining cooking oil from the garlic, then grill (broil) until toasted.

5 Drizzle the walnut oil, if using, over the goat's cheese pâté and generously grind some black pepper over the top.

6 Place a bulb of the baked garlic on to each plate, and serve with the pâté and some of the toasted sourdough bread. Garnish each plate with a few sprigs of fresh thyme and serve a few freshly shelled walnuts and a small bowl of sea salt with each portion.

Nutritional information per portion: Energy 371Kcal/153kJ; Protein 18.52g; Carbohydrate 5,1g, of which sugars3.7g; Fat 32.7g, of which saturates 11.3g; Cholesterol; Calcium 192mg; Fibre 1.7g

Walnut and goat's cheese bruschetta

The combination of toasted walnuts and melting goat's cheese is lovely in this simple appetizer. Walnut bread is readily available in most large supermarkets, and makes an interesting alternative to ordinary crusty bread; although this can be used if walnut bread is unavailable.

SERVES 4

50g/2oz/¹/₂ cup walnut pieces
4 thick slices walnut bread
120ml/4fl oz/¹/₂ cup French dressing
200g/7oz chèvre or other semi-soft
   goat's cheese

1 Preheat the grill (broiler). Lightly toast the walnut pieces, then remove and set aside. Toast the walnut bread on one side. Turn the slices over and drizzle each with 15ml/1 tbsp of the French dressing.

2 Cut the goat's cheese into twelve equal slices and place three on each piece of bread.

3 Grill (broil) the bruschetta for about 3 minutes, until the cheese is melting and beginning to brown.

4 Transfer the bruschetta to serving plates, sprinkle with the toasted walnuts and drizzle with the remaining French dressing. Serve the bruschetta immediately with salad leaves.

Nutritional information per portion: Energy 558Kcal/2321kJ; Protein 16.7g; Carbohydrate 25.6g, of which sugars 2.2g; Fat 37.2g, of which saturates 12.7g; Cholesterol 47mg; Calcium 137mg; Fibre 1.2g; Sodium 841mg.

Cannellini bean bruschetta

This dish is a sophisticated version of beans on toast. Cannellini beans have a delicate flavour and soft texture that melds well with more intense ingredients, such as sun-dried tomatoes, garlic and basil. This makes the perfect summer appetizer or a lazy Sunday brunch dish.

SERVES 4

150g/5oz/²/₃ cup dried cannellini beans, soaked overnight in cold water

5 fresh tomatoes

45ml/3 tbsp olive oil, plus extra for drizzling

2 sun-dried tomatoes in oil, drained and finely chopped

2 garlic cloves

30ml/2 tbsp chopped fresh rosemary

salt and ground black pepper

12 slices Italian-style bread, such as ciabatta

a handful of fresh basil leaves, to garnish

1 Drain and rinse the beans, then place in a pan and cover with fresh water. Bring to the boil and boil rapidly for 10 minutes.

2 Reduce the heat and simmer for 50–60 minutes or until tender. Drain and set aside.

3 Place the tomatoes in a bowl, cover with boiling water, leave for 30 seconds, then peel, seed and chop the flesh.

4 Heat the oil in a frying pan, then add the fresh and sun-dried tomatoes. Crush 1 garlic clove into the pan and add the rosemary. Cook for 2 minutes.

5 Add the tomato mixture to the beans, season and mix. Reheat gently.

6 Cut the remaining garlic in half. Rub the bread with the garlic, then toast. Spoon the bean mixture on to the toast. Sprinkle with basil leaves and drizzle with oil before serving.

Nutritional information per portion: Energy 479kcal/2026kJ; Protein 19.9g; Carbohydrate 74.8g, of which sugars 10.3g; Fat 13.3g, of which saturates 2g; Cholesterol 0mg; Calcium 173mg; Fibre 10.2g; Sodium 563mg.

Asparagus with clarified butter and lemon

Perfect for summer, this light and elegant dish of delicate asparagus drizzled in clarified butter makes a simple and delicious appetizer or side dish, and is ideal for alfresco dining.

SERVES 4

16 white or green asparagus spears
115g/4oz/¹/₂ cup butter, clarified
4 hard-boiled eggs, finely chopped
grated rind and juice of ¹/₂ lemon
salt and ground black or white pepper
a handful of fresh parsley, chopped,
   to garnish

1 Trim the asparagus spears or snap them so that the tender stalk separates from the tougher base. Soak the spears in a bowl of cold water, refreshing the water a couple of times; this makes the stalks more juicy and easier to peel.

2 Bring a large pan of lightly salted water to the boil. Peel the asparagus if necessary, and add the spears to the pan for about 5 minutes.

3 Drain the asparagus and pat dry with kitchen paper. Arrange on individual plates or on a serving platter and cover to keep warm.

4 Heat the clarified butter in a frying pan for about 3 minutes, until pale brown. Add the chopped hard-boiled eggs, and season with salt and pepper. Cook the mixture for 45 seconds, stirring constantly, then add the lemon juice. Pour the mixture over the warm asparagus, sprinkle with the lemon rind and freshly chopped parsley and serve immediately.

Nutritional information per portion: Energy 313kcal/1289kJ; Protein 9.3g; Carbohydrate 2.2g, of which sugars 2.1g; Fat 29.8g, of which saturates 16.6g; Cholesterol 252mg; Calcium 61mg; Fibre 1.7g; Sodium 245mg.

Artichokes with beans and almonds

These tasty artichokes are filled with fresh broad beans and almonds, and flavoured with dill. Prepared artichoke bottoms are available frozen in supermarkets and Middle Eastern stores.

SERVES 4

175g/6oz/2 cups shelled broad
 (fava) beans
4 large globe artichokes, trimmed to
 their bottoms
120ml/4fl oz/¹/₂ cup olive oil
juice of 1 lemon
10ml/2 tsp sugar
75g/3oz/³/₄ cup blanched almonds
1 small bunch of fresh dill, chopped
2 tomatoes, skinned, seeded and diced
salt

1 Put the beans in pan of water and bring to the boil. Lower the heat and simmer for 10–15 minutes or until tender. Drain and refresh under cold running water, then peel off the skins.

2 Place the artichokes in a heavy pan. Mix together the oil, lemon juice and 50ml/2fl oz/¹/₄ cup water and pour over the artichokes. Cover and poach gently for about 20 minutes, then add the sugar, beans and almonds. Cover again and continue to poach gently for a further 10 minutes, or until the artichokes are tender. Toss in half the dill, season with salt, and turn off the heat. Leave the artichokes to cool in the pan.

3 Lift the artichokes out of the pan and place them hollow-side up in a serving dish. Mix the tomatoes with the beans and almonds, spoon into the middle of the artichokes and around them, and garnish with the remaining dill. Serve at room temperature.

Nutritional information per portion: Energy 351kcal/1455kJ; Protein 8.2g; Carbohydrate 13.4g, of which sugars 8.3g; Fat 29.8g, of which saturates 3.6g; Cholesterol 0mg; Calcium 110mg; Fibre 5.5g; Sodium 29mg.

Stuffed vine leaves

For a tasty appetizer to start a vegetarian dinner party, try these vine leaves stuffed with spiced brown rice, nuts and fruit. The filling is infused with sumac, which has a sharp lemon flavour.

SERVES 4–5

20 vacuum-packed vine leaves in brine
90g/3¹/₂oz/¹/₂ cup long grain brown rice
25ml/1¹/₂ tbsp olive oil
1 small onion, finely chopped
50g/2oz/¹/₂ cup pine nuts
45ml/3 tbsp raisins
30ml/2 tbsp chopped fresh mint
2.5ml/¹/₂ tsp ground cinnamon
2.5ml/¹/₂ tsp ground allspice
10ml/2 tsp ground sumac
10ml/2 tsp lemon juice
30ml/2 tbsp tomato purée (paste)
salt and ground black pepper
lemon wedges and mint sprigs, to garnish

1 Rinse the vine leaves well under cold running water. Bring a pan of salted water to the boil. Add the rice, cover and simmer for 10–12 minutes. Drain.

2 Heat 10ml/2 tsp of the olive oil in a frying pan, add the onion and cook until soft. Stir in the pine nuts and cook until lightly browned, then add the raisins, chopped mint, cinnamon, allspice and sumac. Stir in the rice and season to taste.

3 Line a pan with any damaged vine leaves. Trim the stalks from the remaining leaves and lay them flat. Place a little filling on each. Fold the sides over and roll up each leaf neatly. Place the stuffed leaves side by side in the leaf-lined pan.

4 Mix 300ml/¹/₂ pint/1¹/₄ cups water with the lemon juice and tomato purée in a small bowl. Whisk in the remaining olive oil until the mixture is well blended. Pour the mixture over the stuffed vine leaves in the pan, and place a heatproof plate on top to keep them in place.

5 Cover the pan and simmer for 1 hour, until the liquid has been absorbed. Serve the vine leaves hot or cold, garnished with lemon wedges and mint sprigs.

Nutritional information per portion: Energy 43kcal/181kJ; Protein 0.7g; Carbohydrate 6.7g, of which sugars 1.7g; Fat 1.1g, of which saturates 0.1g; Cholesterol 0mg; Calcium 12mg; Fibre 0.3g; Sodium 2mg.

Courgette and feta fritters

Ideal for lunch, supper, a savoury snack or appetizer, these tasty patties are incredibly versatile. You can even make miniature ones and serve them as a nibble with drinks.

SERVES 4–6

3 firm courgettes (zucchini)
30–45ml/2–3 tbsp olive oil
1 large onion, cut in half lengthways, in half again crossways, and sliced along the grain
4 garlic cloves, chopped
45ml/3 tbsp plain (all-purpose) flour
3 eggs, beaten
225g/8oz feta cheese, crumbled
1 bunch each of fresh flat leaf parsley, mint and dill, chopped
5ml/1 tsp Turkish red pepper, or 1 fresh red chilli, seeded and chopped
sunflower oil, for shallow frying
salt and ground black pepper
mint leaves, to garnish

1 Wash the courgettes and trim off the ends. Grate them, then put them in a colander and sprinkle with a little salt. Leave them to weep for 5 minutes.

2 Squeeze the grated courgettes in your hand to extract the juices. Heat the olive oil in a heavy frying pan, stir in the courgettes, onion and garlic and fry until they begin to take on colour. Remove from the heat and leave to cool.

3 Put the flour into a bowl and gradually beat in the eggs to form a smooth batter. Beat in the cooled courgette mixture. Add the feta, herbs and red pepper or chilli, and season with a little pepper. Mix well.

4 Heat enough sunflower oil for shallow frying in a heavy, non-stick pan. Drop four spoonfuls of the mixture into the oil, leaving space between each one, then fry over a medium heat for 6–8 minutes, until firm to the touch and golden on both sides. Remove from the pan and drain on kitchen paper while you fry the remainder. Serve warm, garnished with mint leaves.

Nutritional information per portion: Energy 327kcal/1354kJ; Protein 12.3g; Carbohydrate 12.4g, of which sugars 5.4g; Fat 25.7g, of which saturates 7.9g; Cholesterol 121mg; Calcium 214mg; Fibre 2.3g; Sodium 581mg.

Turkish stuffed aubergines

This sumptuous Turkish meze dish makes an excellent vegetarian appetizer, and can be made ahead as it is served at room temperature. It is traditional to use a lot of olive oil in the preparation of this rich dish, but for a lighter meal you can reduce the amount.

SERVES 4

2 large aubergines (eggplants)
sunflower oil, for shallow frying
1 bunch each of fresh flat leaf parsley
  and dill
1 large onion, halved and finely sliced
3 tomatoes, skinned and finely chopped

2–3 garlic cloves, finely chopped
5ml/1 tsp salt
150ml/$^1/_4$ pint/$^2/_3$ cup olive oil
juice of $^1/_2$ lemon
15ml/1 tbsp sugar
lemon wedges, to serve

1 Peel the aubergines lengthways in stripes like a zebra using a vegetable peeler. Place them in a bowl of salted water for 5 minutes, then drain and pat dry.

2 Heat about 1cm/1/2in sunflower oil in a wok. Place the aubergines in the oil and fry on all sides to soften them. This should take a total of 3–5 minutes. Place them on a chopping board and slit them open lengthways to create pockets, keeping the bottoms and both ends intact so they look like canoes when stuffed.

3 Reserve some dill fronds and parsley for the garnish, then chop the rest and mix them with the onion, tomatoes and garlic. Add the salt and a little of the olive oil. Spoon into the aubergine pockets tightly, so that all of it is used up.

4 Place the filled aubergines side by side in a deep, heavy pan. Mix the remaining olive oil with 50ml/2fl oz/$^1/_4$ cup water and the lemon juice, pour it over the aubergines, and sprinkle the sugar over the top.

5 Cover the pan with its lid and place over a medium heat to get the oil hot and create some steam. Lower the heat and cook the aubergines very gently for about 1 hour, basting from time to time. They should be soft and tender, with only a little oil left in the bottom of the pan.

6 Leave the aubergines to cool in the pan, then carefully transfer them to a serving dish and spoon the oil from the bottom of the pan over them. Garnish with the reserved dill and parsley, and serve at room temperature, with lemon wedges for squeezing.

Nutritional information per portion: Energy 407kcal/1680kJ; Protein 3g; Carbohydrate 16.7g, of which sugars 14.1g; Fat 37g, of which saturates 5.1g; Cholesterol 0mg; Calcium 67mg; Fibre 4.8g; Sodium 507mg.

Grilled aubergine in honey and spices

Hot, spicy, sweet and fruity flavours combine here to send you on an exciting culinary journey. Baby aubergines are very effective for this dish, as you can slice them in half lengthways and hold them by their stalks, making them perfect for sharing.

SERVES 4

2 aubergines (eggplant), peeled and
    thickly sliced
olive oil, for frying
2–3 garlic cloves, crushed
5cm/2in piece of fresh root ginger, peeled
    and grated
5ml/1 tsp ground cumin
5ml/1 tsp harissa
75ml/5 tbsp clear honey
juice of 1 lemon
salt

1 Preheat the grill (broiler) or a griddle. Dip each aubergine slice in olive oil and cook in a pan under the grill or in a griddle pan. Turn the slices so that they are lightly browned on both sides.

2 In a wide frying pan, fry the garlic in a little olive oil for a few seconds, then stir in the ginger, cumin, harissa, honey and lemon juice. Add enough water to cover the base of the pan and to thin the mixture, then lay the aubergine slices in the pan. Cook the aubergines gently for about 10 minutes, or until they have absorbed all the sauce.

3 Add a little extra water, if necessary, season to taste with salt, and serve at room temperature, with chunks of fresh bread to mop up the juices.

Nutritional information per portion: Energy 151Kcal/631kJ; Protein 10.7g; Carbohydrate 9.2g, of which sugars 7g; Fat 34.2g, of which saturates 9.1g; Cholesterol 26mg; Calcium 231mg; Fibre 4.8g; Sodium 608mg.

Crispy golden corn cakes with red pepper aioli

East meets West in these crisp, mouthwatering cakes that bring together creamy goat's cheese and tangy Mediterranean peppers in the Asian wok. If you're short on time, make the piquant aioli using bottled peppers instead of roasting them yourself.

SERVES 4

300g/11oz/scant 2 cups fresh
  corn kernels
200g/7oz/scant 1 cup ricotta cheese
200g/7oz/scant 1 cup goat's
  cheese, crumbled
30ml/2 tbsp thyme leaves
50g/2oz/½ cup plain (all-purpose) flour
1 large (US extra large) egg,
  lightly beaten
150g/5oz natural dried breadcrumbs
vegetable oil, for frying
salt and ground black pepper

FOR THE AIOLI

2 red (bell) peppers, halved and seeded
2 garlic cloves, crushed
250ml/8fl oz/1 cup mayonnaise

1 Make the aioli. Preheat the grill (broiler) to medium-high and cook the peppers, skin-side up, for 8–10 minutes, until the skins blister. Place the peppers in a plastic bag for 10 minutes and then peel away the skin. Place the flesh in a food processor with the garlic and mayonnaise and blend until fairly smooth. Transfer to a bowl and chill.

2 In a bowl, combine the corn, cheeses and thyme, then stir in the flour and egg and season well.

3 Place the breadcrumbs on a plate. Roll 15ml/1 tbsp of the corn mixture into a ball, flatten slightly and coat in the breadcrumbs. Place on baking parchment and chill for 30 minutes.

4 Fill a wok one-third full of oil and heat to 180°C/350°F (or until a cube of bread browns in 45 seconds). Working in batches, deep-fry the corn cakes for 1–2 minutes, until golden. Drain well on kitchen paper and serve with the aioli.

Nutritional information per portion: Energy 1048kcal/4363kJ; Protein 26.1g; Carbohydrate 68.2g, of which sugars 17.3g; Fat 76.5g, of which saturates 22g; Cholesterol 162mg; Calcium 156mg; Fibre 3.9g; Sodium 1091mg.

Spicy corn patties

Easy to eat with your fingers, these corn patties are delicious served with fresh lime wedges and a small dollop of chilli sambal on the side to give them an extra fiery kick.

SERVES 4

2 fresh corn on the cob

3 shallots, chopped

2 garlic cloves, chopped

25g/1oz galangal or fresh root
   ginger, chopped

1–2 chillies, seeded and chopped

2–3 candlenuts or macadamia
   nuts, ground

5ml/1 tsp ground coriander

5ml/1 tsp ground cumin

15ml/1 tbsp coconut oil

3 eggs

45–60ml/3–4 tbsp grated fresh coconut or
   desiccated (dry unsweetened
   shredded) coconut

2–3 spring onions (scallions), white parts
   only, finely sliced

corn or groundnut (peanut) oil, for
   shallow frying

salt and ground black pepper

1 small bunch fresh coriander (cilantro)
   leaves, roughly chopped, to serve

1 lime, quartered, to serve

chilli sambal, for dipping

1 Put the corn into a large pan of water, bring to the boil and cook for about 8 minutes, until cooked but still firm. Drain the cobs and refresh under running cold water. Using a sharp knife, scrape all the corn off the cob and put aside.

2 Using a mortar and pestle, grind the shallots, garlic, galangal and chillies to a paste. Add the ground nuts, ground coriander and cumin and beat well together.

3 Heat the coconut oil in a small wok or heavy pan, stir in the spice mixture and stir-fry until it becomes fragrant and begins to colour. Transfer the mixture to a plate and leave to cool.

4 Beat the eggs in a large bowl. Add the coconut and spring onions, and beat in the corn and the cooled spice mixture until thoroughly combined. Season the mixture with salt and pepper.

5 Heat a layer of corn oil in a frying pan. Working in batches, drop spoonfuls of the corn mixture into the oil and fry the patties for 2–3 minutes, until golden on both sides. Drain the patties and serve them with the coriander leaves, wedges of lime to squeeze over them and a chilli sambal for dipping.

Nutritional information per portion: Energy 368kcal/1531kJ; Protein 10.8g; Carbohydrate 18.1g, of which sugars 8.2g; Fat 28.7g, of which saturates 9.7g; Cholesterol 143mg; Calcium 68mg; Fibre 4.1g; Sodium 196mg

Courgette fritters

A healthier twist on Japanese tempura, which uses Indian spices and gram flour – made from chickpeas – in the batter. The result is a wonderful snack that has a light, crispy coating, while the courgette baton inside becomes meltingly tender.

SERVES 4

90g/3½oz/¾ cup gram flour
5ml/1 tsp baking powder
2.5ml/½ tsp ground turmeric
10ml/2 tsp ground coriander
5ml/1 tsp ground cumin
5ml/1 tsp chilli powder
250ml/8fl oz/1 cup bottled beer
600g/1lb 6oz courgettes (zucchini), cut
    into batons
sunflower oil, for deep-frying
sea salt
steamed basmati rice, soya yogurt and
    pickles, to serve

1 Sift the gram flour, baking powder, turmeric, coriander, cumin and chilli powder into a large bowl. Stir lightly to mix through.

2 Season the mixture with salt and then gradually add the beer, mixing gently as you pour it in, to make a thick batter – be careful not to overmix.

3 Fill a large wok or deep, heavy pan one-third full with sunflower oil and heat to 180°C/350°F or until a cube of bread, dropped into the oil, browns in about 45 seconds.

4 Working in batches, dip the courgette batons in the batter and then deep-fry for 1–2 minutes until crisp and golden. Lift out of the wok using a slotted spoon. Drain on kitchen paper and keep warm.

5 Serve immediately with steamed basmati rice, soya yogurt and pickles.

Nutritional information per portion: Energy 207kcal/857kJ; Protein 8.3g; Carbohydrate 10.8g, of which sugars 4.7g; Fat 14.8g, of which saturates 2.4g; Cholesterol 95mg; Calcium 104mg; Fibre 2.1g; Sodium 50mg.

Roasted courgettes and peaches with pine nuts

This recipe combines fruit and vegetables to make a colourful medley that is baked rather than deep-fried or grilled. It can be served with a yogurt or tarator sauce, or a tahini dressing. It is ideal as an appetizer with warm, crusty bread, or as an accompaniment to a larger meal.

SERVES 4

2 courgettes (zucchini)

2 yellow or red (bell) peppers, seeded and
   cut into wedges

100ml/3½ fl oz/scant ½ cup olive oil

4–6 plum tomatoes

2 firm peaches, peeled, halved and stoned
   (pitted), then cut into wedges

30ml/2 tbsp pine nuts

salt and ground black pepper

FOR THE YOGURT SAUCE

500g/1¼ lb/2¼ cups thick and creamy
   natural (plain) yogurt

2–3 garlic cloves, crushed

juice of ½ lemon

1 Preheat the oven to 200°C/400°F/ Gas 6. Peel the courgettes lengthways in stripes like a zebra, then halve and slice them lengthways.

2 Place the courgettes and peppers in a baking dish. Drizzle the oil over them and sprinkle with salt, then bake in the oven for 20 minutes. Take the dish out of the oven and turn the vegetables in the oil, then mix in the tomatoes and peaches. Bake for another 20–25 minutes, until everything is nicely browned.

3 Meanwhile, make the yogurt sauce. In a bowl, beat the yogurt with the garlic and lemon juice. Season with salt and pepper and set aside.

4 Dry-roast the pine nuts in a small, heavy pan until they turn golden brown and give off a nutty aroma. Remove from the heat.

5 When the roasted vegetables are ready, remove the dish from the oven and sprinkle the pine nuts over the top. Serve with the yogurt sauce.

Nutritional information per portion: Energy 362kcal/1507kJ; Protein 11.7g; Carbohydrate 26.7g, of which sugars 26.3g; Fat 24.1g, of which saturates 3.7g; Cholesterol 2mg; Calcium 284mg; Fibre 4.8g; Sodium 120mg.

Pea and potato pakoras with coconut and mint chutney

These delicious golden bites make a wonderful snack drizzled with the fragrant chutney, sandwiched in a crusty roll for a light lunch.

MAKES 25

15ml/1 tbsp sunflower oil
20ml/4 tsp cumin seeds
5ml/1 tsp black mustard seeds
1 small onion, finely chopped
10ml/2 tsp grated fresh root ginger
2 green chillies, seeded
   and chopped
600g/1lb 5oz potatoes, peeled, diced and
   boiled until tender
200g/7oz fresh peas
juice of 1 lemon
90ml/6 tbsp chopped fresh coriander
   (cilantro) leaves
vegetable oil, for frying
salt and ground black pepper

FOR THE BATTER

115g/4oz/1 cup besan (chickpea flour)
25g/1oz/¼ cup self-raising (self-rising) flour
40g/1½oz/⅓ cup rice flour
large pinch of turmeric
10ml/2 tsp crushed coriander seeds
350ml/12fl oz/1½ cups water

FOR THE CHUTNEY

105ml/7 tbsp coconut cream
200ml/7fl oz/scant 1 cup natural
   (plain) yogurt
50g/2oz mint leaves, finely chopped
5ml/1 tsp golden caster (superfine) sugar
juice of 1 lime

1 Heat a wok over a medium heat and add the sunflower oil. When hot, add the cumin and mustard seeds and stir-fry for 1–2 minutes.

2 Add the onion, ginger and chillies to the wok and cook for 3–4 minutes. Add the cooked potatoes and peas and stir-fry for 3–4 minutes. Season, then stir in the lemon juice and coriander leaves.

3 Leave the mixture to cool slightly, then divide into 25 portions. Shape each portion into a ball and chill.

4 To make the batter put the besan, self-raising flour and rice flour in a bowl. Season and add the turmeric and coriander seeds. Gradually whisk in the water to make a smooth, thick batter.

5 To make the chutney place all the ingredients in a blender and process until smooth. Season with salt and pepper, then chill.

6 To cook the pakoras, fill a wok one-third full of oil and heat to 180°C/350°F. (A cube of bread, dropped into the oil, should brown in 45 seconds.) Working in batches, dip the balls in the batter, then drop into the oil and deep-fry for 1–2 minutes, or until golden. Drain on kitchen paper and serve with the chutney.

Nutritional information per portion: Energy 126Kcal/525kJ; Protein 4.1g; Carbohydrate 8.3g, of which sugars 2.6g; Fat 8.8g, of which saturates 5.2g; Cholesterol 0mg; Calcium 35mg; Fibre 1.3g; Sodium 16mg.

Chive dumplings

These dumplings are lovely and light, thanks to the wheat starch flour used for the wrappers. Although there is an art to making them, the end result is well worth the effort. Try to find the Chinese chives used in this recipe as they will add extra crunch and flavour.

SERVES 6–8

150g/5oz/1¼ cups wheat starch
200ml/7fl oz/scant 1 cup water
15ml/1 tbsp vegetable oil
50g/2oz/½ cup tapioca flour
pinch of salt
sesame oil, for brushing
chilli sauce, to serve

FOR THE FILLING

200g/7oz Chinese chives
30ml/2 tbsp light soy sauce
15ml/1 tbsp sesame oil
2.5ml/½ tsp ground black pepper
15ml/1 tbsp cornflour (cornstarch)
1 egg, lightly beaten

1 Put the wheat starch in a non-stick pan. Add the water and oil and cook over a low heat, stirring occasionally, until very thick. Remove from the heat and leave to cool.

2 Meanwhile, prepare the filling. Chop the chives finely. Put them in a bowl and stir in the soy sauce, sesame oil, pepper and cornflour. Heat a wok, add the mixture and toss over a low heat for 5 minutes. Stir in the lightly beaten egg, then set it aside.

3 Stir the tapioca flour and salt into the cool wheat starch mixture. Mix well, then transfer to a floured board. Knead for at least 5 minutes.

4 Roll out the dough thinly and stamp out into 12 circles, 7.5cm/3in in diameter.

5 Place 1 heaped tablespoon of the chive filling on each dough circle and fold in half to make half-moon shapes. Seal the edges with a little water. Brush each dumpling with a little sesame oil to prevent them from sticking to each other when being steamed.

6 Place the dumplings in a steamer and cook them for 10 minutes. Place the dumplings on a serving plate and serve immediately, accompanied by a chilli sauce dip.

Nutritional information per portion: Energy 140kcal/589kJ; Protein 1.8g; Carbohydrate 25.9g, of which sugars 0.9g; Fat 3.9g, of which saturates 0.6g; Cholesterol 24mg; Calcium 58mg; Fibre 1.3g; Sodium 295mg.

Beansprout and cucumber parcels

These delightful rice paper rolls filled with crunchy raw summer vegetables, fresh mint and coriander are healthy and refreshing, either as a snack or an appetizer to a meal. As well as being vegetarian these are gluten-free, making them ideal for those who cannot eat wheat.

SERVES 4

12 round rice papers

1 medium lettuce, leaves separated and ribs removed

2–3 carrots, cut into julienne strips

1 small cucumber, peeled, halved lengthways and seeded, and cut into julienne strips

3 spring onions (scallions), trimmed and cut into julienne strips

225g/8oz mung beansprouts

1 small bunch fresh mint leaves, roughly chopped

1 small bunch fresh coriander (cilantro) leaves, roughly chopped

dipping sauce, to serve

1 Pour some lukewarm water into a shallow dish. Soak the rice papers, two or three at a time, for 5 minutes until pliable. Place the soaked papers on a clean dish towel and cover with a second dish towel to keep them moist.

2 Work with one paper at a time. Place a lettuce leaf toward the edge nearest to you, leaving about 2.5cm/1in to fold over. Place a mixture of the vegetables on top, followed by some mint and coriander leaves.

3 Fold the edge nearest to you over the filling, tuck in the sides, and roll tightly to the edge on the far side. Place the filled roll on a plate and cover with clear film (plastic wrap), so it does not dry out. Repeat with the remaining rice papers and vegetables.

4 Serve the rolls with a dipping sauce of your choice. If you are making these ahead of time, keep them in the refrigerator under a damp dish towel, so that they remain moist.

Nutritional information per portion: Energy 105kcal/441kJ; Protein 4g; Carbohydrate 20g, of which sugars 6.6g; Fat 1g, of which saturates 0.2g; Cholesterol 0mg; Calcium 74mg; Fibre 3.7g; Sodium 23mg.

Salads

Fresh, vibrant and full of flavour, a salad can make any meal an event. This chapter includes some classic, as well as more unusual vegetarian salads, featuring a plethora of exotic and varied ingredients. Treat yourself to a luxurious Wild Mushroom Salad, enjoy the festive flavours of a Sauerkraut Salad with Cranberries or transport yourself to a tropical idyll with a Celery and Coconut Salad with Lime.

Classic tomato salad

It is important to use perfectly ripe tomatoes for this deliciously ripe salad that is bursting with the tastes of summer. They should be full-flavoured and firm enough to slice neatly with a serrated knife. You can peel the tomatoes before slicing them, but it is not strictly necessary.

SERVES 4

4 ripe but firm tomatoes on the vine
2–3 shallots, finely chopped
45ml/3 tbsp chopped fresh parsley or dill
30ml/2 tbsp red wine vinegar
90ml/6 tbsp vegetable oil, olive oil or
 a mixture
salt and ground black pepper

1 Remove the stem and core from each tomato, then slice them evenly and arrange them neatly on a serving platter.

2 Sprinkle with the shallots, season with salt and pepper and sprinkle with the chopped parsley or dill.

3 Make a simple dressing by putting the vinegar in a bowl and whisking in the oil. Drizzle the dressing over the tomatoes.

4 Cover with clear film (plastic wrap) and marinate for 30 minutes at room temperature before serving.

Nutritional information per portion: Energy 171kcal/705kJ; Protein 1.1g; Carbohydrate 3.9g, of which sugars 3.5g; Fat 16.9g, of which saturates 2g; Cholesterol 0mg; Calcium 34mg; Fibre 1.6g; Sodium 11mg.

Bread and tomato salad

This famous Italian salad has a substantial bread base with the addition of tomatoes, onions, cucumbers and basil to give it flavour and freshness. It is a rustic dish, perfect for hot summer days, and is a useful way of using up leftover bread, which needs to be coarse and crusty.

SERVES 4

8 slices casareccio-type bread or
   ciabatta, stale
4 beefsteak tomatoes, chopped
1 large red onion, chopped
1 large cucumber, chopped
a handful of fresh basil leaves, torn
   into pieces
extra virgin olive oil, to taste
red wine vinegar, to taste
sea salt and ground black pepper

1 Soak the bread in cold water for about 15 minutes, then squeeze the bread dry in a clean dish towel.

2 Mix the damp bread with the tomatoes, onion, cucumber and basil.

3 Dress the salad with with olive oil, vinegar and salt and pepper to taste.

4 Toss the salad ingredients together thoroughly and leave it to stand for about 30 minutes before serving.

Nutritional information per portion: Energy 238kcal/998kJ; Protein 5.3g; Carbohydrate 28g, of which sugars 5.9g; Fat 12.5g, of which saturates 1.9g; Cholesterol 0mg; Calcium 116mg; Fibre 3.2g; Sodium 259mg.

Wild mushroom salad

If picking wild mushrooms to make this salad, you must make sure that the mushrooms are edible, and also that they are safe to eat raw. It is important to slice the mushrooms as thinly as possible and to eat them soon after preparation so that they don't shrivel up.

SERVES 4

**500g/1¼lb mixed wild or
    cultivated mushrooms**
200g/7oz Parmesan cheese
**a large handful of fresh flat leaf parsley
    leaves, finely chopped**
juice of ½ lemon
extra virgin olive oil, to drizzle
sea salt and ground black pepper

1 Clean and trim the mushrooms carefully. Do not wash them, but use a brush to clean off any traces of soil.

2 Once clean, slice the mushrooms very thinly. Shave the Parmesan as thinly as possible.

3 Arrange the sliced mushrooms on a large platter, then sprinkle the chopped parsley and Parmesan shavings over the top.

4 Sprinkle with lemon juice, drizzle with oil and season. Serve within half an hour.

Nutritional information per portion: Energy 247kcal/1027kJ; Protein 22.3g; Carbohydrate 0.9g, of which sugars 0.5g; Fat 17.2g, of which saturates 10.4g; Cholesterol 50mg; Calcium 633mg; Fibre 2g; Sodium 556mg.

Warm spring cabbage salad

A very simple recipe for a warm cabbage salad. As with all recipes that rely on very few, basic ingredients, it is important that the flavourings, in this case the red wine vinegar, should be of the best possible quality – strong and tasty as well as sharp and sour.

SERVES 4

1 large spring cabbage
300ml/¹/₂ pint/1¹/₄ cups extra virgin olive oil
100ml/3¹/₂ fl oz/scant ¹/₂ cup red wine vinegar
3 garlic cloves, lightly crushed
sea salt and ground black pepper

1 Remove the hard outer leaves of the cabbage. Shred the rest of the cabbage finely and put it into a colander. Rinse it well several times, then drain thoroughly.

2 Pour the oil and vinegar into a pan over a medium heat. Add the garlic. Heat until sizzling.

3 Transfer the shredded cabbage to a salad bowl, then pour over the hot garlic oil. Toss the mixture together thoroughly.

4 Season with salt and pepper, toss again and cover with a plate to allow it to steam for about 2–3 minutes. Serve.

Nutritional information per portion: Energy 484kcal/1991kJ; Protein 1.9g; Carbohydrate 6.2g, of which sugars 5.6g; Fat 50.2g, of which saturates 7g; Cholesterol 0mg; Calcium 56mg; Fibre 2.5g; Sodium 8mg.

Potato and feta salad

This potato salad is redolent with the aromas of the herbs and has layer upon layer of flavours. It is an easy dish to assemble, so makes a perfect lunch or dinner for a busy day. Serve it on its own, or as a second course to a bean or lentil based soup. Look for a flavoursome salad potato like Charlotte, as this will make all the difference.

SERVES 4

500g/1¼lb small new potatoes

5 spring onions (scallions), green and white parts, finely chopped

15ml/1 tbsp rinsed bottled capers

8–10 black olives

115g/4oz feta cheese, cut into small cubes

45ml/3 tbsp finely chopped fresh flat leaf parsley

30ml/2 tbsp finely chopped fresh mint

salt and ground black pepper

FOR THE VINAIGRETTE

90–120ml/6–8 tbsp extra virgin olive oil

juice of 1 lemon, or to taste

2 salted or preserved anchovies, rinsed and finely chopped

45ml/3 tbsp Greek (US strained plain) yogurt

45ml/3 tbsp finely chopped fresh dill

5ml/1 tsp French mustard

1 Bring a pan of lightly salted water to the boil and cook the potatoes in their skins for 25–30 minutes, until tender. Take care not to let them become overcooked and disintegrate. Drain them thoroughly and let them cool a little.

2 When the potatoes are cool enough to handle, peel them and place in a large bowl. If they are very small, keep them whole; otherwise cut them into large cubes. Add the spring onions, capers, olives, feta and fresh herbs and toss gently to mix.

3 To make the vinaigrette, place the oil in a bowl with the lemon juice and anchovies.

4 Whisk thoroughly until the dressing emulsifies and thickens. Whisk in the yogurt, dill and mustard, with salt and pepper to taste.

5 Dress the salad while the potatoes are still warm, tossing lightly to coat everything in the delicious anchovy vinaigrette.

Nutritional information per portion: Energy 138Kcal/566kJ; Protein 1.3g; Carbohydrate 1.2g, of which sugars 1.1g; Fat 14.2g, of which saturates 2g; Cholesterol 0mg; Calcium 75mg; Fibre 1.4g; Sodium 419mg.

Cabbage salad with lemon vinaigrette and olives

White cabbage tends to be a little woody, but produces a sweet tasting, unusual salad. Here it is drizzled with a lemon dressing to produce a delightfully crisp and refreshing dish.

SERVES 4

1 white cabbage
12 black olives

FOR THE VINAIGRETTE
75–90ml/5–6 tbsp extra virgin olive oil
30ml/2 tbsp lemon juice
1 garlic clove, crushed
**30ml/2 tbsp finely chopped fresh flat
   leaf parsley**
salt

1 Cut the cabbage in quarters, discard the outer leaves and trim off any thick, hard stems as well as the hard base.

2 Lay each quarter on its side and cut long, very thin slices until you reach the central core, which should be discarded. The key to a perfect cabbage salad is to shred the cabbage as finely as possible.

3 Place the cabbage in a bowl and stir in the black olives, these can be stoned (pitted) if preferred.

4 Make the vinaigrette by whisking the olive oil, lemon juice, garlic, parsley and salt together in a bowl until well blended. Pour the dressing over the salad, and toss the cabbage and olives until everything is evenly coated. Serve immediately.

Nutritional information per portion: Energy 307Kcal/1269kJ; Protein 3.9g; Carbohydrate 12.8g, of which sugars 12.5g; Fat 26.9g, of which saturates 3.8g; Cholesterol 0mg; Calcium 145mg; Fibre 5.8g; Sodium 21mg.

Leek and red pepper salad with goat's cheese

The contrasting textures of silky, grilled peppers, soft cheese and slightly crisp leeks makes this salad especially delicious. This makes a good first course served with crusty bread.

SERVES 6

4 x 1cm/½in thick slices French goat's
   cheese log (chèvre)
65g/2½oz/1 cup fine dry white
   breadcrumbs
675g/1½lb young slender
   leeks, trimmed
15ml/1 tbsp olive oil
2 large red peppers
few sprigs fresh thyme, chopped
vegetable oil, for shallow frying
45ml/3 tbsp chopped fresh flat
   leaf parsley
salt and ground black pepper

FOR THE DRESSING

75ml/5 tbsp extra virgin olive oil
1 small garlic clove, finely chopped
5ml/1 tsp Dijon mustard, plain or
   flavoured with herbes de Provence
15ml/1 tbsp red wine vinegar

1 Remove any skin from the cheese and roll the slices in the breadcrumbs, pressing them in so that the cheese is well coated. Chill for 1 hour.

2 Cook the leeks in boiling salted water for 3–4 minutes. Drain and cut into 7.5–10cm/3–4in lengths. Toss in the oil, seasoning to taste. Grill the leeks for 3 minutes on each side.

3 Halve and seed the peppers, then grill them, skin side uppermost, until the skin is blackened and blistered. Place them in a bowl, cover and leave to stand for 10 minutes, so that they soften in their own steam.

4 Remove the skin from the peppers and cut the flesh into strips, then mix with the leeks and thyme.

5 Make the dressing by whisking all the ingredients together in a bowl, seasoning to taste. Pour the dressing over the salad and chill.

6 When ready to serve, heat a shallow layer of vegetable oil in a frying pan and fry the cheese until golden brown on each side. Drain on kitchen paper and cool slightly, then cut into bitesize pieces. Toss the cheese and parsley into the salad and serve immediately.

Nutritional information per portion: Energy 265Kcal/1100kJ; Protein 5.7g; Carbohydrate 17g, of which sugars 6.5g; Fat 19.7g, of which saturates 3.9g; Cholesterol 8mg; Calcium 60mg; Fibre 3.7g; Sodium 174mg.

Sauerkraut salad with cranberries

In this recipe the distinctive flavours of tart pickled cabbage and cranberries are combined with sweet apple to create an elegant sweet and sour salad that is packed with flavour and is very healthy. This looks and tastes very festive, so is the perfect for Christmas time.

SERVES 4–6

500g/1¼lb sauerkraut

2 red apples

100–200g/3¾–7oz/scant 1–1¾ cups
   fresh cranberries or lingonberries

30ml/2 tbsp sugar

60–75ml/4–5 tbsp sunflower oil

2–3 sprigs fresh parsley, to garnish

1 Put the sauerkraut in a colander and drain thoroughly. Taste, and if you find it is too sour, rinse it under cold running water then drain well.

2 Put the sauerkraut in a large bowl. Slice or cut the apples into slices or wedges. Add the apples and the cranberries or lingonberries to the sauerkraut. Sprinkle over the sugar, pour the oil on top and mix all the ingredients well together.

3 To serve, turn the sauerkraut into a serving bowl and garnish with the parsley sprigs.

Nutritional information per portion: Energy 105kcal/437kJ; Protein 1.3g; Carbohydrate 8.8g, of which sugars 8.8g; Fat 7.4g, of which saturates 0.9g; Cholesterol 0mg; Calcium 49mg; Fibre 3.1g; Sodium 493mg.

Summer salad with salad cream dressing

Homemade salad cream, such as the one in this recipe, makes a delicious alternative to mayonnaise and vinaigrette, and tastes much better than store-bought versions. For a slightly sharper finish to the dressing, try replacing the cream with crème fraîche.

SERVES 4

2 hard-boiled eggs
15ml/1 tbsp caster (superfine) sugar
2.5ml/½ tsp salt
15ml/1 tbsp Swedish or German mustard
30ml/2 tbsp lemon juice
200ml/7fl oz/scant 1 cup double
    (heavy) cream
summer salad leaves, such as little
    gem lettuce
½ cucumber, sliced
15ml/1 tbsp chopped fresh chives or dill

1 Cut the hard-boiled eggs in half, remove the egg yolks and reserve the whites. Push the yolks through a sieve (strainer) into a bowl, then add the sugar, salt, mustard and lemon juice and blend together.

2 Whisk the cream in a bowl until it begins to thicken but is not stiff. Add to the egg mixture and mix to form a creamy dressing.

3 Arrange the salad leaves and cucumber slices on four individual serving plates and spoon over the salad cream. Chop the reserved egg whites and scatter over the top with the chopped herbs.

Nutritional information per portion: Energy 315kcal/1302kJ; Protein 4.8g; Carbohydrate 6.7g, of which sugars 6.6g; Fat 30.2g, of which saturates 17.5g; Cholesterol 164mg; Calcium 60mg; Fibre 0.5g; Sodium 405mg.

White bean salad with red pepper dressing

The speckled herb and red pepper dressing adds a wonderful colour contrast to this salad, which is best served warm. Canned beans are used for convenience.

SERVES 4

1 large red (bell) pepper
60ml/4 tbsp olive oil
1 large garlic clove, crushed
25g/1oz/1 cup fresh oregano leaves or
   flat leaf parsley
15ml/1 tbsp balsamic vinegar
2 x 400g/14oz cans flageolet (small
   cannellini) beans, drained and rinsed
400g/14oz can cannellini beans, drained
   and rinsed
salt and ground black pepper

1 Preheat the oven to 200°C/400°F/ Gas 6. Place the red pepper on a baking sheet, brush with a little of the oil and roast for 30 minutes or until the skin wrinkles and the flesh is soft.

2 Remove the pepper from the oven and place in a plastic bag. Seal and leave to cool.

3 When the pepper is cool enough to handle, remove it from the bag and peel off the skin. Rinse under cold running water. Slice the pepper in half, remove the seeds and dice. Set aside.

4 Heat the remaining olive oil in a frying pan and cook the crushed garlic for 1 minute until softened, but now brown. Remove from the heat, then add the oregano or parsley, the red pepper and any juices, and the balsamic vinegar and combine.

5 Put the beans in a large serving bowl and pour over the dressing. Mix well.

6 Season the salad to taste, then stir gently until well combined. Serve warm.

Nutritional information per portion: Energy 267kcal/1117kJ; Protein 11.1g; Carbohydrate 29.8g, of which sugars 8.3g; Fat 12.2g, of which saturates 1.8g; Cholesterol 0mg; Calcium 133mg; Fibre 10.6g; Sodium 591mg.

Tofu and wild rice salad

The flavours in this salad are influenced by the cuisines of North Africa and the Mediterranean. It goes well with chargrilled vegetables, such as red onions, tomatoes and peppers.

SERVES 4

175g/6oz/scant 1 cup basmati rice
50g/2oz/generous ¼ cup wild rice
250g/9oz firm tofu, drained and cubed
25g/1oz preserved lemon, finely chopped
20g/¾oz bunch of parsley, chopped

FOR THE DRESSING
1 garlic clove, crushed
10ml/2 tsp clear honey
10ml/2 tsp of the preserved lemon juice
15ml/1 tbsp balsamic vinegar
15ml/1 tbsp olive oil
1 small fresh red chilli, seeded and
    finely chopped
5ml/1 tsp harissa paste (optional)
sea salt and ground black pepper

1 Cook the basmati rice and the wild rice in separate pans until tender. The basmati will take about 10–15 minutes to cook while the wild rice should take about 45–50 minutes. Drain, rinse under cold water and drain again, then place in a large bowl together.

2 Meanwhile whisk together all the dressing ingredients in a small bowl. Add the tofu, stir to coat and leave to marinate while the rice cooks.

3 Gently fold the marinated tofu, dressing, preserved lemon and parsley into the rice, check the seasoning and serve.

VARIATION
Look for rose harissa paste, which is available from the special range in some large supermarkets or from delicatessens or food halls. It is coloured with rose petals, and is exceptionally delicious when used in this recipe, and still fiery hot.

Nutritional information per portion: Energy 286kcal/1195kJ; Protein 9.8g; Carbohydrate 48g, of which sugars 2.4g; Fat 5.8g, of which saturates 0.7g; Cholesterol 0mg; Calcium 355mg; Fibre 0.7g; Sodium 7mg.

Egg and fennel tabbouleh with nuts

Tabbouleh is a well-known and popular Middle Eastern salad of bulgur wheat, flavoured with lots of parsley, mint, lemon juice and garlic. This variation of the classic dish has the same basic ingredients but also includes the distinctive aniseed flavour of fennel.

SERVES 4

250g/9oz/1¼ cups bulgur wheat

4 small (US medium) eggs

1 fennel bulb

1 bunch of spring onions (scallions), chopped

25g/1oz/½ cup drained sun-dried tomatoes
    in oil, sliced

45ml/3 tbsp chopped fresh parsley

30ml/2 tbsp chopped fresh mint

75g/3oz/½ cup black olives

60ml/4 tbsp olive oil

30ml/2 tbsp garlic oil

30ml/2 tbsp lemon juice

50g/2oz/½ cup chopped
    hazelnuts, toasted

pitta bread, warmed, to serve

salt and ground black pepper

1 Place the bulgur wheat in a bowl; pour in boiling water to cover and leave to soak for about 15 minutes.

2 Drain the bulgur wheat in a metal sieve (strainer), and place the sieve over a pan of boiling water. Cover the pan and sieve with a lid and steam for about 10 minutes. Fluff up the grains with a fork and spread out on a metal tray. Set aside to cool.

3 Hard-boil the eggs for 8 minutes. Cool under running water, peel and quarter, or, using an egg slicer, slice not quite all the way through.

4 Halve and finely slice the fennel. Boil in salted water for 6 minutes, drain and cool under running water.

5 Combine the eggs, fennel, spring onions, sun-dried tomatoes, parsley, mint and olives with the bulgur wheat. Dress with olive oil, garlic oil and lemon juice and sprinkle with the hazelnuts. Season well and serve with pitta bread.

Nutritional information per portion: Energy 512kcal/2129kJ; Protein 15.7g; Carbohydrate 50.9g, of which sugars 2.8g; Fat 28g, of which saturates 4.1g; Cholesterol 190mg; Calcium 135mg; Fibre 3.9g; Sodium 509mg.

Warm black-eyed bean salad with rocket

This is easy to prepare, as black-eyed beans do not need to be soaked overnight. By adding spring onions and plenty of aromatic dill, it is transformed into a refreshing and healthy dish. Serve hot or at room temperature, depending on your preference.

SERVES 4

275g/10oz/1¹/₂ cups black-eyed
   beans (peas)
5 spring onions (scallions), sliced
a large handful of rocket (arugula) leaves,
   chopped if large
45–60ml/3–4 tbsp chopped fresh dill
150ml/¹/₄ pint/²/₃ cup extra virgin
   olive oil
juice of 1-2 lemons, to taste
10–12 black olives
salt and ground black pepper
small cos or romaine lettuce leaves,
   to serve

1 Rinse and drain the beans, transfer them to a pan and pour in cold water to cover. Bring to the boil and immediately drain. Put them back in the pan with fresh cold water to cover and add a pinch of salt – this will stop them from disintegrating as they cook.

2 Bring the beans to the boil, then lower the heat and cook until they are soft but not mushy. They will take 20–30 minutes.

3 Drain the beans, reserving 75–90ml/5–6 tbsp of the cooking liquid. Transfer the beans to a large salad bowl.

4 Immediately add the spring onions, rocket, dill, olive oil, lemon juice, olives and reserved liquid. Season to taste and mix well.

5 Serve the salad immediately, or allow to cool room temperature and serve piled on the lettuce leaves.

Nutritional information per portion: Energy 238Kcal/1007kJ; Protein 16.1g; Carbohydrate 31g, of which sugars 2.4g; Fat 6.4g, of which saturates 0.9g; Cholesterol 0mg; Calcium 114mg; Fibre 12.3g; Sodium 580mg.

Lentil salad with red onion and garlic

This delicious, garlicky lentil salad is superb served as an accompaniment to vegetable kebabs at a barbecue, or as a dinner party appetizer. It can be served warm or cooled, and with a generous spoonful of yogurt for a refreshing variation.

SERVES 4

45ml/3 tbsp olive oil

2 red onions, chopped

2 tomatoes, peeled, seeded and chopped

10ml/2 tsp ground turmeric

10ml/2 tsp ground cumin

175g/6oz/³⁄₄ cup brown or green lentils, picked over and rinsed

900ml/1¹⁄₂ pints/3³⁄₄ cups vegetable stock or water

4 garlic cloves, crushed

small bunch of fresh coriander (cilantro), finely chopped

salt and ground black pepper

1 lemon, cut into wedges, to serve

1 Heat 30ml/2 tbsp of the oil in a large pan or flameproof casserole and fry the onions until soft. Add the tomatoes, turmeric and cumin, then stir in the lentils. Pour in the stock or water and bring to the boil, then reduce the heat and simmer until the lentils are tender and almost all the liquid has been absorbed.

2 In a separate pan, fry the garlic in the remaining oil until brown and crispy. Toss the garlic into the lentils with the fresh coriander and season to taste.

3 Serve the salad warm or at room temperature, with wedges of lemon for squeezing over.

Nutritional information per portion: Energy 244Kcal/1025kJ; Protein 12.3g; Carbohydrate 29.2g, of which sugars 6.6g; Fat 9.5g, of which saturates 1.3g; Cholesterol 0mg; Calcium 78mg; Fibre 6.1g; Sodium 16mg.

Gypsy salad with feta, chillies and parsley

This tempting meze salad is packed full of Mediterranean flavours, and is based on the classic Turkish combination of chopped cucumber, tomatoes, peppers, onion and flat leaf parsley. This is heightened by the addition of deliciously salty, crumbled feta cheese.

SERVES 3–4

2 red onions, cut in half lengthways and finely sliced along the grain
1 green (bell) pepper, seeded and sliced
1 fresh green chilli, seeded and chopped
2–3 garlic cloves, chopped
1 bunch of flat leaf parsley, chopped
225g/8oz firm feta cheese, crumbled
2 large tomatoes, skinned, seeded and finely chopped
30–45ml/2–3 tbsp olive oil
salt and ground black pepper
5ml/1 tsp red pepper flakes, to garnish

1 Sprinkle the onions with a little salt to draw out the juice. Leave for about 10 minutes, then rinse and pat dry.

2 Put the onions and green pepper in a bowl with the chilli, garlic, parsley, feta and tomatoes.

3 Add the oil and seasoning and toss well.

4 Transfer the salad to a large serving dish and sprinkle over the red pepper flakes before serving.

Nutritional information per portion: Energy 253kcal/1049kJ; Protein 11.1g; Carbohydrate 13.4g, of which sugars 11g; Fat 17.6g, of which saturates 8.6g; Cholesterol 39mg; Calcium 260mg; Fibre 3.2g; Sodium 824mg.

Sautéed herb salad with preserved lemon

Firm-leafed fresh herbs, such as flat leaf parsley and mint, tossed in a little olive oil and seasoned with salt, are fabulous to serve as a salad in a meze spread or go wonderfully with spicy tagines. Lightly sautéed with garlic and served warm with yogurt, this dish is delightful even on its own.

SERVES 4

large bunch of flat leaf parsley
large bunch of mint
large bunch of fresh coriander (cilantro)
bunch of rocket (arugula)
large bunch of spinach leaves (about 115g/4oz)
60–75ml/4–5 tbsp olive oil
2 garlic cloves, finely chopped
1 green or red chilli, seeded and finely chopped
1/2 preserved lemon, finely chopped
salt and ground black pepper
45–60ml/3–4 tbsp Greek (US strained plain) yogurt, to serve

1 Roughly chop the herbs, rocket and spinach.

2 Heat the olive oil in a wide, heavy pan. Stir in the garlic and chilli, and fry until they begin to colour.

3 Toss in the herbs, rocket and spinach and cook gently, until they begin to soften and wilt. Add the preserved lemon and season to taste. Serve the salad warm with a spoonful of yogurt.

VARIATION

For a spicier dressing try crushing a clove of garlic and stirring it into the yogurt with salt and ground pepper to taste.

Nutritional information per portion: Energy 157Kcal/647kJ; Protein 2.9g; Carbohydrate 1.6g, of which sugars 1.5g; Fat 15.6g, of which saturates 2.6g; Cholesterol 0mg; Calcium 135mg; Fibre 2.1g; Sodium 70mg.

Quinoa salad with mango

Since quinoa has a mild, slightly bitter taste, it is best when combined with ingredients that have a more robust flavour, such as fresh herbs, chilli, fruit and nuts, as in this super-healthy salad. You could serve this salad with slices of griddled halloumi cheese.

SERVES 4

130g/4½ oz quinoa
1 mango
60ml/4 tbsp pine nuts
large handful fresh basil, roughly chopped
large handful fresh flat leaf parsley,
   roughly chopped
large handful fresh mint, roughly chopped

1 mild long fresh red chilli, seeded
   and chopped

FOR THE DRESSING

1 tbsp lemon juice
1 tbsp extra virgin olive oil
salt and ground black pepper

1 Put the quinoa in a pan and cover with cold water. Season with salt and bring to the boil. Reduce the heat, cover the pan with a lid and simmer for 12 minutes or until the quinoa is tender. Drain well.

2 Meanwhile, prepare the mango. Cut vertically down each side of the stone (pit). Taking the two large slices, cut the flesh into a criss-cross pattern down to, but not through, the skin.

3 Press each half inside out, then cut the mango cubes away from the skin.

4 Toast the pine nuts for a few minutes in a dry frying pan until golden, then remove from the heat.

5 Mix together the ingredients for the dressing and season well.

6 Transfer the cooked quinoa to a bowl and add the herbs and chilli. Pour the dressing over the quinoa and fork lightly until combined. Season to taste and transfer to a serving dish or four individual dishes. Arrange the mango on top of the herby quinoa and sprinkle with the pine nuts.

Nutritional information per portion: Energy 206Kcal/857kJ; Protein 4.5g; Carbohydrate 23.1g, of which sugars 6.2g; Fat 11.2g, of which saturates 1g; Cholesterol 0mg; Calcium 62mg; Fibre 2.5g; Sodium 9mg.

Artichoke heart and orange salad

This colourful, fruity salad will please the eye and refresh the palate after a spicy dish. When fresh artichokes are not readily available, opt for the frozen hearts that can be found in some supermarkets.

SERVES 4

1 lemon, halved
4 artichoke hearts
4 Seville (Temple) oranges
6 red radishes, finely sliced
12 kalamata olives
30–45ml/2–3 tbsp olive oil
salt
2.5ml/¹/₂ tsp paprika, to serve

1 Squeeze the juice from ¹/₂ lemon and pour into a pan. Add the artichoke hearts and plenty of water to cover. Bring to the boil, then reduce the heat and simmer gently for about 15 minutes until just tender.

2 Drain and refresh the hearts under cold running water, then drain again. Slice the artichoke hearts thickly and place them in a bowl.

3 Peel the oranges with a knife, cutting off all the pith. Cut between the membranes into the centre to remove the segments of fruit. Discard any pips and add the segments to the artichoke hearts.

4 Add the radishes and olives, drizzle with the olive oil and the juice from the remaining ¹/₂ lemon, and carefully mix the salad. Season with salt and paprika before serving.

Nutritional information per portion: Energy 243Kcal/1007kJ; Protein 2.1g; Carbohydrate 12g, of which sugars 12g; Fat 21.1g, of which saturates 3g; Cholesterol 0mg; Calcium 112mg; Fibre 3.6g; Sodium 0mg.

Globe artichoke salad

Globe artichokes are a real treat for the eye as well as the palate. This salad makes a versatile and elegant first course, and is equally good when served hot or cold.

SERVES 4

4 artichokes
juice of 1 lemon
900ml/1½ pints/3¾ cups half home-
   made vegetable stock and half water
2 garlic cloves, chopped
1 small bunch parsley
6 whole peppercorns
15ml/1 tbsp olive oil, plus extra
   for drizzling

1 Trim the stalks of the artichokes close to the base, cut the very tips off the leaves and then divide them into quarters. Remove the inedible hairy chokes (the central parts), carefully scraping the hairs away from the heart at their bases.

2 Squeeze a little of the lemon juice over the cut surfaces of the artichokes to prevent discoloration.

3 Put the artichokes into a pan and cover with the stock and water, garlic, parsley, peppercorns and olive oil. Cover and cook gently for 1 hour.

4 Remove the artichokes and keep them warm if serving hot. Boil the cooking liquor rapidly without the lid, to reduce by half, and then strain.

5 To serve, arrange in small serving dishes and pour over the reduced juices. Drizzle over a little extra olive oil and lemon juice. Provide finger bowls and a large bowl for the leaves.

6 To eat, pull a leaf away from the artichoke and scrape the fleshy part at the base with your teeth. Discard the remainder of the leaves and then eat the heart at the base.

Nutritional information per portion: Energy 59Kcal/245kJ; Protein 0.7g; Carbohydrate 7.8g, of which sugars 7.3g; Fat 3.1g, of which saturates 0.5g; Cholesterol 0mg; Calcium 25mg; Fibre 2.4g; Sodium 61mg.

Aubergine salad with tahini dressing

This is a deliciously smoky salad that balances sweet and sharp flavours. It makes a good filling for pitta bread, with some crisp lettuce and sweet, ripe tomatoes.

SERVES SIX

3 aubergines (eggplants), cut into 1cm/½in
    thick slices
675g/1½lb onions, thickly sliced
75–90ml/5–6 tbsp olive oil
5ml/1 tsp powdered sumac (optional)
45ml/3 tbsp chopped flat leaf parsley
45ml/3 tbsp pine nuts, toasted
salt and ground black pepper

FOR THE DRESSING

2 garlic cloves, crushed
150ml/¼ pint/⅔ cup light tahini
juice of 1–2 lemons, to taste
45–60ml/3–4 tbsp water

1 Place the aubergines on a rack or in a colander, and sprinkle generously with salt. Leave for 45–60 minutes, then rinse under cold running water and pat dry with kitchen paper.

2 Thread the onions on to skewers or place them in an oiled wire grill cage.

3 Brush the aubergines and onions with about 45ml/3 tbsp of the oil and grill for 6–8 minutes on each side. Brush with more oil, if necessary, when you turn the vegetables. The vegetables should be browned and soft when cooked. The onions may need a little longer than the aubergines.

4 Arrange the vegetables on a serving dish and sprinkle with the sumac, if using, and season with salt and pepper to taste. Sprinkle with the remaining oil if they seem dry.

5 For the dressing, crush the garlic in a mortar with a pinch of salt and gradually work in the tahini. Gradually work in the juice of 1 lemon, followed by the water. Taste and add more lemon juice if you think the dressing needs it. Thin with more water, if necessary, so that the dressing is fairly runny.

6 Drizzle the dressing over the salad and leave for 30–60 minutes, then sprinkle with the chopped parsley and pine nuts. Serve immediately at room temperature, not chilled.

Nutritional information per portion: Energy 344kcal/1423kJ; Protein 8.2g; Carbohydrate 11.8g, of which sugars 8.9g; Fat 29.8g, of which saturates 3.8g; Cholesterol 0mg; Calcium 226mg; Fibre 6.1g; Sodium 13mg.

Beetroot with lemon dressing

Fresh beetroot is a real summer treat, when it is widely enjoyed and used more often than the pickled form more familiar throughout the rest of the year. This simple salad makes the most of the beetroot's robust flavour and makes a delicious and colourful addition to an alfresco lunch.

SERVES 4

450g/1lb evenly-sized raw
   beetroot (beets)
grated rind and juice of 1/2 lemon
about 150ml/1/4 pint/2/3 cup extra virgin
   olive oil (or a mixture of olive and
   sunflower oil, blended to taste)
sea salt and ground black pepper
chopped fresh chives, to
   garnish (optional)

1 Twist off the tops from the beetroot and cook in a large pan of salted boiling water for 30 minutes.

2 Pinch the skin between two fingers: when cooked, the skin will come away easily. Drain the beetroot and allow it to cool.

3 Peel the beetroot and slice it into wedges. Place it into a bowl and add the lemon rind and juice, and the oil.

4 Season, mix the salad to coat the beetroot in the lemon and oil mixture, garnish with the chives, if using, and serve immediately.

Nutritional information per portion: Energy 265Kcal/1097kJ; Protein 1.9g; Carbohydrate 8.6g, of which sugars 7.9g; Fat 25.1g, of which saturates 3.6g; Cholesterol 0mg; Calcium 23mg; Fibre 2.2g; Sodium 74mg.

Beetroot salad with oranges

This salad can be made with bought vacuum-packed cooked beetroot or freshly steamed or boiled vegetables. The combination of sweet beetroot, zesty orange and warm cinnamon is both unusual and delicious, and this dish provides a lovely burst of colour in a summer buffet spread.

SERVES 4–6

675g/1½lb beetroot (beet), steamed or
   boiled, then peeled
1 orange, peeled and sliced
30ml/2 tbsp orange flower water
15ml/1 tbsp sugar
5ml/1 tsp ground cinnamon
salt and ground black pepper

1 Quarter the cooked beetroot, then slice the quarters. Arrange on a plate with the orange slices.

2 Gently heat the orange flower water with the sugar, stir in the cinnamon and season to taste. Pour the sweet mixture over the beetroot and orange salad and chill for at least 1 hour before serving.

COOK'S TIP

When cooking raw beetroot, always leave the skin on and trim off only the tops of the leaf stalks. Cook the beetroot in boiling water or steam over rapidly boiling water for 1–2 hours, depending on their size. Small beetroot are tender in about 1 hour, medium roots take 1–1½ hours, and larger roots can take up to 2 hours.

Nutritional information per portion: Energy 58Kcal/247kJ; Protein 2.2g; Carbohydrate 12.9g, of which sugars 12.2g; Fat 0.1g, of which saturates 0g; Cholesterol 0mg; Calcium 33mg; Fibre 2.5g; Sodium 75mg.

Fried tofu salad with a tangy sauce

This Malaysian salad is spicy and refreshing, and makes an ideal accompaniment to grilled vegetables and stir-fried noodles. The beansprouts and crushed peanuts add a delightful crunch to the salad, and the tamarind, a vibrant fruity sweetness. Kecap manis is a sweet soy sauce that is thickened with palm sugar (jaggery) and should be available in Asian food stores.

SERVES 4

vegetable oil, for deep-frying
450g/1lb firm rectangular tofu, rinsed,
    patted dry and cut into blocks
1 small cucumber, partially peeled in strips,
    seeded and shredded
2 spring onions (scallions), trimmed, halved
    and shredded
2 handfuls of fresh beansprouts rinsed
    and drained
fresh coriander (cilantro) leaves,
    to garnish

FOR THE SAUCE

30ml/2 tbsp tamarind pulp, soaked
    in water
15ml/1 tbsp sesame oil
4 shallots, finely chopped
4 garlic cloves, finely chopped
2 red chillies, seeded
115g/4oz/1 cup roasted
    peanuts, crushed
30–45ml/2–3 tbsp kecap manis
15ml/1 tbsp tomato ketchup

1 First make the sauce. Squeeze the tamarind pulp to soften it in the water, and then strain through a sieve (strainer). Measure out 120ml/4fl oz/$\frac{1}{2}$ cup tamarind pulp.

2 Heat the oil in a wok and stir in the shallots, garlic and chillies, until fragrant. Stir in the peanuts, until they emit a nutty aroma. Add the kecap manis, tomato ketchup and tamarind pulp and blend to form a thick sauce. Set aside and leave to cool.

3 Heat enough oil for deep-frying in a wok or heavy pan. Lower in the blocks of tofu and fry until golden brown all over. Pat dry on kitchen paper and cut each block into strips.

4 Arrange the strips on a plate with the cucumber, spring onions and beansprouts. Drizzle the sauce over the top or serve it separately in a bowl, and garnish with the coriander leaves.

Nutritional information per portion: Energy 423Kcal/1749kJ; Protein 17.9g; Carbohydrate 7.8g, of which sugars 4.5g; Fat 35.8g, of which saturates 5.3g; Cholesterol 0mg; Calcium 607mg; Fibre 2.8g; Sodium 296mg.

Celery and coconut salad with lime

This salad is unusual in its use of grated coconut, which is usually reserved as a garnish for sweet dishes. Juicy and refreshing, it is welcome on a hot sunny day as part of a buffet spread outdoors, or as an accompaniment to grilled or barbecued vegetables and spicy dishes. It looks especially appealing when served in coconut shell halves.

SERVES 3–4

45–60ml/3–4 tbsp natural (plain) yogurt

2 garlic cloves, crushed

5ml/1 tsp grated lime zest

juice of 1 lime

8 long celery sticks, grated (leaves reserved for the garnish)

flesh of ½ fresh coconut, grated

salt and ground black pepper

a few sprigs of fresh flat leaf parsley, to garnish

1 Mix the yogurt and garlic in a bowl, add the lime rind and juice and season with salt and pepper.

2 Fold in the grated celery and coconut, then set aside for 15–20 minutes to let the celery juices weep. Don't leave it for too long or it will become watery.

3 To serve, spoon the salad into a bowl and garnish with celery leaves and sprigs of parsley.

COOK'S TIP
To grate coconut flesh you may find it useful to use the grating disc of a food processor. The flesh will keep in the refrigerator for up to 2 days.

Nutritional information per portion: Energy 126kcal/521kJ; Protein 2.1g; Carbohydrate 2.9g, of which sugars 2.9g; Fat 11.9g, of which saturates 10.1g; Cholesterol 0mg; Calcium 63mg; Fibre 3.6g; Sodium 69mg.

Rojak

Originally from Indonesia, rojak is found in several Asian cuisines. The Chinese, Peranakans and Malays all have their own versions, varying from region to region, but all include a selection of fruit and vegetables, bathed in a tangy sauce. As this recipe is so flexible, you can really use any combination or fruit and vegetables, and make the sauce as pungent and fiery as you like.

SERVES 4–6

1 jicama (sweet turnip), peeled and
   finely sliced
1 small cucumber, peeled and finely sliced
1 green mango, peeled and finely sliced
1 star fruit (carambola), finely sliced
4 slices fresh pineapple, cored
half a pomelo, separated into segments,
   with membrane removed
a handful of beansprouts, rinsed
fresh mint leaves, to garnish

FOR THE SAUCE

225g/8oz/2 cups roasted peanuts
4 garlic cloves, chopped
2–4 red chillies, seeded and chopped
20ml/4 tsp tamarind paste
30ml/2 tbsp palm sugar (jaggery)
salt

1 Start by making the sauce. Using a mortar and pestle or a food processor, grind the roasted peanuts with the chopped garlic and chillies to a coarse paste.

2 Beat in tamarind paste and palm sugar. Add enough water to make a thick, pouring sauce, and stir the mixture until the sugar has dissolved. Add salt to taste.

3 Arrange the sliced fruit and vegetables on a serving plate, with the beansprouts sprinkled generously over the top.

4 Drizzle the peanut and tamarind sauce over the top of the vegetables and garnish the salad with mint leaves. Serve with grilled vegetables and spicy dishes, or on its own as a healthy snack.

Nutritional information per portion: Energy 330Kcal/1381kJ; Protein 12.9g; Carbohydrate 28g, of which sugars 25.1g; Fat 19.3g, of which saturates 3.4g; Cholesterol 13mg; Calcium 114mg; Fibre 6.3g; Sodium 416mg.

Noodle, tofu and sprouted bean salad

This crisp and refreshing salad is quick to make, and is bursting with the goodness of fresh vegetables and the fragrant flavour of herbs, rice vinegar and spicy chilli oil. Fresh sprouted beans are available from most supermarkets, but you can easily sprout them yourself at home.

SERVES 4

25g/1oz bean thread noodles

500g/1¼lb mixed sprouted beans and
pulses (aduki, chickpea, mung, red lentil)

4 spring onions (scallions),
finely shredded

115g/4oz firm tofu, diced

1 ripe plum tomato, seeded and diced

½ cucumber, peeled, seeded and diced

60ml/4 tbsp chopped fresh
coriander (cilantro)

45ml/3 tbsp chopped fresh mint

60ml/4 tbsp rice vinegar

10ml/2 tsp caster (superfine) sugar

10ml/2 tsp sesame oil

5ml/1 tsp chilli oil

salt and ground black pepper

1 Place the bean thread noodles in a bowl and pour over enough boiling water to cover. Leave to soak for 12–15 minutes and then drain and refresh under cold, running water and drain again.

2 Using a pair of scissors, cut the noodles roughly into 7.5cm/3in lengths and put into a bowl.

3 Fill a wok one-third full of boiling water and place over a high heat.

4 Add the beans and pulses to the wok and blanch for about 1 minute. Drain, transfer to the noodle bowl, and add the spring onions, tofu, tomato, cucumber and herbs.

5 Combine the rice vinegar, sugar, sesame and chilli oils and toss into the noodle mixture.

6 Transfer the coated noodles to a serving dish and chill for 30 minutes before serving.

Nutritional information per portion: Energy 126Kcal/528kJ; Protein 7.2g; Carbohydrate 14.8g, of which sugars 7.2g; Fat 4.4g, of which saturates 0.6g; Cholesterol 0mg; Calcium 209mg; Fibre 3.1g; Sodium 17mg.

Green papaya salad

Throughout South-east Asia, unripe green mangoes and papayas are used for salads. Their tart, crunchy flesh complements spicy stir-fried dishes beautifully. This Filipino version is sweet and sour, achieving a balance that goes perfectly with grilled or roasted vegetables.

SERVES 4

2 green papayas, seeded and grated
4 shallots, finely sliced
1–2 red chillies, seeded, halved
    lengthways and finely sliced
150g/5oz/1 cup plump sultanas (golden
    raisins) or raisins
2 garlic cloves, crushed
25g/1oz fresh root ginger, grated
45–60ml/3–4 tbsp coconut vinegar
50g/2oz palm sugar (jaggery)
coriander (cilantro) sprigs, to garnish

1 Put the papaya, shallots, chillies, sultanas or raisins, garlic and ginger into a bowl. In a separate small bowl, mix together the coconut vinegar and sugar until the sugar has completely dissolved.

2 Pour the sweet vinegar over the salad and toss well together.

3 Set the salad aside to marinate for at least 1 hour or, for the best flavour, in the refrigerator overnight to allow the flavours to mingle. Serve garnished with coriander leaves.

VARIATION
Use green mango or grated carrots, for their vibrant colours.

Nutritional information per portion: Energy 232kcal/988kJ; Protein 2.5g; Carbohydrate 58.3g, of which sugars 57.6g; Fat 0.4g, of which saturates 0g; Cholesterol 0mg; Calcium 81mg; Fibre 5.5g; Sodium 19mg.

Main Meals

From comforting pies through to delicately spiced curries, this chapter features delicious meat-free main dishes for every occasion and from all corners of the globe. Revel in the sun-drenched flavours of the Mediterranean with Spinach and Ricotta Ravioli, take a fragrant and exotic journey to the East with Jewelled Vegetable Rice with Crispy Eggs or settle down with a warming and traditional Potato and Leek Filo Pie.

Swiss chard pie

The deliciously flaky pastry of this pie conceals a tasty garlic and nutmeg-scented filling of eggs and super-healthy Swiss chard. Any kind of Swiss chard will work well, but for extra colour and vibrance you could seek out the red-stemmed variety.

SERVES 8

FOR THE FILLING:
1kg/2¼lb Swiss chard, thickly sliced
45ml/3 tbsp vegetable oil
1 small red onion, finely chopped
2 garlic cloves, chopped
2.5ml/½ tsp grated nutmeg
2.5ml/½ tsp salt
1.5ml/½ tsp black pepper
4 eggs
3 hard-boiled eggs

FOR THE PASTRY:
500g/1¼lb self-raising (self-rising) flour,
   plus extra for dusting
5ml/1 tsp salt
130g/4½oz margarine
75ml/5 tbsp water
1 egg yolk, lightly beaten

1 To make the filling, blanch the Swiss chard in boiling water for 5 minutes then drain well and set aside.

2 Heat the oil in a pan over a medium heat and fry the onion and garlic for 5 minutes until softened and starting to brown. Stir in the Swiss chard, nutmeg, salt and pepper and continue to cook for 3 minutes, then remove from the heat and leave to cool.

3 To make the pastry, sift the flour and salt into a bowl, then rub in the margarine using your fingers or two forks. Add the water and draw the pastry together with your fingers. Knead lightly to form a smooth dough and leave to rest in a cool place for 10 minutes.

4 Preheat the oven to 180°C/350°F/Gas 4 and oil a rectangular baking tray, 25 x 15cm/10 x 6in. Divide the dough into two pieces, one larger than the other.

5 On a floured surface, thinly roll out the larger piece of pastry and use to line the tray, leaving the edges of the pastry hanging over the sides.

6 Beat the 4 eggs lightly together and stir them into the cooled filling. Pour the mixture into the pastry-lined tray. Cut the hard-boiled eggs in half and press them into the filling, distributing them evenly. Dampen the edges of the pastry.

7 Roll out the remaining dough and cover the pie, sealing the edges by pressing them together with your fingers. Trim the edges and cut out decorations for the top from the pastry trimmings if you wish.

8 Brush the surface of the pie with the egg yolk and bake for about 45 minutes until the pastry is crisp and golden brown. Leave to cool before serving.

Nutritional information per portion: Energy 274kcal/1138kJ; Protein 9g; Carbohydrate 11g, of which sugars 1.7g; Fat 21.9g, of which saturates 13.4g; Cholesterol 95mg; Calcium 83mg; Fibre 0.6g; Sodium 131mg.

Red onion tart with a cornmeal crust

Red onions are mild and sweet when cooked, and combine well with fontina cheese and thyme in this tart. Cornmeal gives the pastry a crumbly texture to contrast with the juiciness of the filling.

SERVES 5–6

60ml/4 tbsp olive oil

1kg/2¼lb red onions, thinly sliced

2–3 garlic cloves, thinly sliced

5ml/1 tsp chopped fresh thyme, plus a few whole sprigs, to garnish

5ml/1 tsp soft dark brown sugar

10ml/2 tsp sherry vinegar

225g/8oz fontina cheese, thinly sliced

salt and ground black pepper

FOR THE PASTRY

115g/4oz/1 cup plain (all-purpose) flour

75g/3oz/¾ cup fine yellow cornmeal

5ml/1 tsp soft dark brown sugar

5ml/1 tsp chopped fresh thyme

90g/3½oz/7 tbsp butter

1 egg yolk

30–45ml/2–3 tbsp iced water

1 To make the pastry, sift the flour and cornmeal into a bowl with 5ml/1 tsp salt. Stir in the sugar and thyme, then rub in the butter until the mixture resembles breadcrumbs. Beat the egg yolk with 30ml/2 tbsp iced water and bind the pastry, adding another 15ml/1 tbsp iced water, if needed. Gather the dough into a ball, wrap in clear film (plastic wrap) and chill for 30–40 minutes.

2 Heat 45ml/3 tbsp of oil in a frying pan and add the onions. Cover and cook, stirring occasionally, for 25 minutes. Add the garlic and thyme, then cook for 10 minutes. Increase the heat slightly, then add the sugar and vinegar. Cook, uncovered, for 5 minutes, until the onions start to caramelize. Season, then cool.

3 Preheat the oven to 190°C/375°F/Gas 5. Roll out the pastry thinly and line a 25cm/10in loose-based metal flan tin (pan). Prick all over with a fork and support the sides with foil. Bake for 12–15 minutes, until lightly coloured. Remove the foil and spread the onions over the base of the pastry case. Add the fontina and sprigs of thyme and season. Drizzle over the remaining oil, then bake for 20 minutes, until piping hot. Garnish with thyme and serve.

Nutritional information per portion: Energy 494Kcal/2051kJ; Protein 13.2g; Carbohydrate 38.9g, of which sugars 11.3g; Fat 31.7g, of which saturates 16g; Cholesterol 100mg; Calcium 172mg; Fibre 3.2g; Sodium 307mg.

Puff pastry cabbage pie

Crisp puff pastry with a deliciously soft and buttery cabbage filling makes a warming treat when served with creamy mashed potatoes and simple vegetables. Perfect for chilly winter nights.

SERVES 4–6

300–400g/11–14oz cabbage
40–50g/1¹/₂–2oz/3–4 tbsp butter
3 eggs
1 sheet ready-made chilled puff pastry,
    measuring about 40x20cm/16x8in
salt

FOR THE GLAZE
1 egg yolk
5ml/1 tsp water
15ml/1 tbsp fresh white breadcrumbs

1 Discard the outer leaves and stalk of the cabbage, and chop finely. Heat the butter in a frying pan, add the cabbage and stir-fry for 25 minutes until soft.

2 Put the eggs in a pan, cover with cold water and bring to the boil. Reduce the heat, and simmer for 10 minutes, then drain. Remove the shells from the eggs then chop and put in a large bowl. Add the cabbage to the bowl and mix.

3 Preheat the oven to 220°C/425°F/ Gas 7. Put the sheet of pastry on a dampened baking tray. Spread the cabbage and egg mixture lengthways on one half of the pastry sheet. Brush the edges with water and fold the other side over to enclose. Seal together by pressing with a fork along the join.

4 Whisk together the egg yolk and water. Brush the pastry with the mixture and make some small holes in the top with a fork. Sprinkle the breadcrumbs over.

5 Bake the pie in the oven for 12–15 minutes, until the pastry is crisp and golden brown. Cut into portions and serve.

Nutritional information per portion: Energy 333kcal/1388kJ; Protein 7.9g; Carbohydrate 25.3g, of which sugars 3.3g; Fat 23.6g, of which saturates 4.5g; Cholesterol 143mg; Calcium 80mg; Fibre 1.2g; Sodium 276mg.

Ratatouille and fontina strudel

Mix a colourful jumble of ratatouille vegetables with chunks of creamy fontina cheese, then wrap in sheets of filo and bake for a delicious, summer-party pastry.

SERVES 6

1 small aubergine (eggplant), diced
45ml/3 tbsp extra virgin olive oil
1 onion, sliced
2 garlic cloves, crushed
1 red (bell) pepper, cored and sliced
1 yellow (bell) pepper, cored and sliced
2 courgettes (zucchini), cut into
    small chunks
generous pinch of dried mixed herbs
30ml/2 tbsp pine nuts
30ml/2 tbsp raisins
8 sheets of filo pastry, each measuring 30
    x 18cm/12 x 7in, thawed if frozen
50g/2oz/¼ cup butter, melted
130g/4½oz/generous 1 cup diced
    Fontina cheese
salt and ground black pepper
mixed salad, to serve

1 Layer the diced aubergine in a colander, sprinkling each layer with salt. Drain over the sink for 20 minutes, then rinse well and pat dry.

2 Heat the oil in a frying pan, add the onion, garlic, peppers and aubergine and fry over a low heat, stirring occasionally, for about 10 minutes until golden. Add the courgettes, herbs and salt and pepper. Cook for 5 minutes until softened. Cool to room temperature, then stir in the pine nuts and raisins.

3 Preheat the oven to 180°C/350°F/Gas 4. Brush two sheets of filo pastry with a little of the melted butter. Lay the filo sheets side by side, overlapping them slightly by about 5cm/2in, to make a large rectangle. Cover with the remaining filo sheets, brushing each layer with melted butter. Spoon the vegetable mixture down one long side of the filo.

4 Sprinkle the cheese on top, then roll up and transfer to a non-stick baking sheet, curling the roll round in a circle. Brush with the remaining butter. Bake for 30 minutes, cool for 10 minutes, then slice and serve with mixed salad.

Nutritional information per portion: Energy 327Kcal/1359kJ; Protein 8.7g; Carbohydrate 22.8g, of which sugars 9.6g; Fat 22.4g, of which saturates 9.5g; Cholesterol 38mg; Calcium 106mg; Fibre 2.9g; Sodium 178mg.

Cheese and spinach flan

The decorative pastry topping for this flan is made using a lattice cutter. If you don't have one, cut the pastry into fine strips and weave them into a lattice yourself.

SERVES 8

450g/1lb frozen spinach
1 onion, chopped
pinch of grated nutmeg
225g/8oz/1 cup cottage cheese
2 large eggs
50g/2oz Parmesan cheese, grated
150ml/¼ pint/⅔ cup single (light) cream
1 egg, beaten
salt and ground black pepper

FOR THE PASTRY

225g/8oz/2 cups plain (all-purpose) flour, plus extra for dusting
115g/4oz/½ cup butter
2.5ml/½ tsp English (hot) mustard
2.5ml/½ tsp paprika
115g/4oz Cheddar cheese, finely grated
45–60ml/3–4 tbsp chilled water

1 To make the pastry, sift the flour into a bowl and rub in the butter. Stir in the mustard powder, paprika, salt and cheese. Bind the dough with the water. Knead until smooth, wrap in clear film (plastic wrap) and chill for 30 minutes.

2 Cook the spinach and onion in a pan until soft. Season with salt, pepper and nutmeg. Put into a bowl and add the cheeses, eggs and cream. Mix well.

3 Preheat the oven to 200°C/400°F/Gas 6. Put a baking sheet in the oven to preheat. Roll out two-thirds of the pastry on a lightly floured surface and use to line a 23cm/9in loose-based flan tin (pan). Press the pastry into the edges and make a narrow lip around the top edge. Spoon the filling into the flan case.

4 Roll out the remaining pastry and cut it with a lattice pastry cutter. Lay it over the flan. Brush the edges with beaten egg, press together and trim off the excess. Brush the top of the flan with egg and bake on the baking sheet for 35–40 minutes, until golden. Serve hot or cold.

Nutritional information per portion: Energy 401Kcal/1674kJ; Protein 17.5g; Carbohydrate 24.1g, of which sugars 2.4g; Fat 26.4g, of which saturates 15.6g; Cholesterol 147mg; Calcium 374mg; Fibre 2.2g; Sodium 389mg.

Mediterranean one-crust pie

This rustic pie encases a rich tomato, aubergine and kidney bean filling. If your pastry cracks, just patch it up – a rough appearance adds to the pie's character.

SERVES 4

500g/1¼lb aubergine (eggplant), cubed
1 red (bell) pepper
30ml/2 tbsp olive oil
1 large onion, finely chopped
1 courgette (zucchini), sliced
2 garlic cloves, crushed
15ml/1 tbsp chopped fresh oregano
200g/7oz can red kidney beans, rinsed
115g/4oz/1 cup pitted black olives, rinsed
150ml/¼ pint/⅔ cup passata (bottled strained tomatoes)
1 egg, beaten, or a little milk
30ml/2 tbsp semolina
salt and ground black pepper

FOR THE PASTRY

75g/3oz/⅔ cup plain (all-purpose) flour
75g/3oz/⅔ cup wholemeal (whole-wheat) flour
75g/3oz/6 tbsp vegetable margarine
50g/2oz/⅔ cup grated Parmesan cheese
60–90ml/4–6 tbsp chilled water

1 Preheat the oven to 220°C/425°F/Gas 7. To make the pastry, sift the flours into a bowl and rub in the margarine, then stir in the Parmesan. Mix in enough water to form a dough. Chill for 30 minutes.

2 On a floured surface, knead the dough into a ball. Wrap in clear film (plastic wrap) and chill for 30 minutes.

3 Sprinkle the aubergine with salt in a colander and leave for 30 minutes. Rinse and pat dry. Roast the red pepper in the oven for 20 minutes. Put the pepper in a plastic bag. When cool, remove, peel and seed, then dice the flesh. Set aside.

4 Fry the onion in the olive oil for 5 minutes, until soft. Add the aubergine and fry for 5 minutes more. Add the courgette, garlic and oregano. Cook for 5 minutes more, stirring often. Add the kidney beans, olives and passata, stir and season to taste. Cook until heated through, then set aside.

5 Roll out the pastry to a rough 30cm/12in round. Place on a lightly oiled baking sheet. Brush with beaten egg or milk, sprinkle with semolina, leaving a 4cm/1½in border, then spoon over the filling. Fold up the pastry edges, leaving the middle open. Brush the pastry with the remaining egg and bake for 30–35 minutes.

Nutritional information per portion: Energy 554Kcal/2318kJ; Protein 17.7g; Carbohydrate 56.6g, of which sugars 15.7g; Fat 30.2g, of which saturates 4.2g; Cholesterol 13mg; Calcium 295mg; Fibre 11.6g; Sodium 1353mg.

Spicy potato strudel

Here, a tasty mixture of vegetables, cooked in a spicy, creamy sauce, is wrapped in crisp filo pastry. Serve with a good selection of chutneys or a yogurt and mint sauce.

SERVES 4

65g/2½oz/5 tbsp butter
1 onion, chopped
2 carrots, coarsely grated
1 courgette (zucchini), chopped
350g/12oz firm potatoes, chopped
10ml/2 tsp mild curry paste
2.5ml/½ tsp dried thyme
150ml/¼ pint/⅔ cup water
1 egg, beaten
30ml/2 tbsp single (light) cream
50g/2oz/½ cup grated Cheddar cheese
8 sheets of filo pastry, thawed if frozen
sesame seeds, for sprinkling
salt and ground black pepper

1 Melt 25g/1oz/2 tbsp of the butter in a frying pan and cook the onion, carrots, courgette and potatoes for 5 minutes, tossing them to ensure they cook evenly. Stir in the curry paste and continue to cook the vegetables for 1–2 minutes more until tender.

2 Add the thyme, water and seasoning. Bring to the boil, then reduce the heat and simmer for 10 minutes until tender, stirring occasionally. Set aside to cool.

3 Transfer the vegetable mixture to a large bowl, then mix in the egg, cream and cheese. Chill until you are ready to fill the filo pastry.

4 Preheat the oven to 190°C/375°F/ Gas 5. Melt the remaining butter and lay out four sheets of filo pastry, slightly overlapping them to form a large rectangle. Brush with some melted butter and lay the other sheets on top. Brush with more butter.

5 Spoon the filling along one long side of the pastry, then roll it up. Form it into a circle and place on a baking sheet. Brush with the remaining butter and sprinkle over the sesame seeds.

6 Bake for about 25 minutes, or until golden and crisp. Leave the strudel to stand for 5 minutes before cutting into slices and serving.

Nutritional information per portion: Energy 362Kcal/1512kJ; Protein 9.8g; Carbohydrate 34.8g, of which sugars 6.5g; Fat 21.1g, of which saturates 12.7g; Cholesterol 98mg; Calcium 169mg; Fibre 3g; Sodium 227mg.

Potato and leek filo pie

This filo pastry pie would make an attractive and impressive centrepiece for a vegetarian buffet. This dish is best served cold, accompanied by a selection of salads.

SERVES 8

800g/1¾lb new potatoes

2 large leeks

75g/3oz/6 tbsp butter

15g/½oz/½ cup fresh parsley, finely chopped

60ml/4 tbsp chopped mixed fresh herbs

12 sheets of filo pastry, thawed if frozen

150g/5oz Cheshire or Lancashire cheese, sliced

2 garlic cloves, finely chopped

250ml/8fl oz/1 cup double (heavy) cream

2 large (US extra large) egg yolks

salt and ground black pepper

1 Preheat the oven to 190°C/375°F/ Gas 5. Slice the potatoes and cook them in a pan of salted boiling water for 3–4 minutes, then drain and set aside.

2 Trim the leeks and rinse them under cold running water. Drain them, then slice thinly.

3 Melt 25g/1oz/2 tbsp of the butter in a frying pan, add the sliced leeks and fry, stirring occasionally, until softened.

4 Remove from the heat, season with pepper and stir in half the parsley and half the mixed herbs. Set the pan aside.

5 Melt the remaining butter in a pan. Line a deep 23cm/9in loose-based cake tin (pan) with 6–7 sheets of filo pastry, lightly brushing each layer with butter. Let the edges of the pastry overhang the tin.

6 Layer the potatoes, leek mixture and cheese in the tin, sprinkling some of the herbs and all the garlic between each of the layers. Season each with salt and plenty of pepper.

7 Fold the overhanging pastry over the filling and cover with 2 sheets of filo, tucking in the sides to fit. Brush with melted butter. Cover the pie loosely with foil and bake for 35 minutes. (Keep the remaining sheets of filo pastry covered with clear film (plastic wrap) and a damp dishtowel.)

8 Meanwhile, in a small bowl, beat the cream, egg yolks and remaining chopped herbs together. Remove the foil from the pie, make a hole in the centre of the pastry and gradually pour in the egg and cream mixture.

9 Lower the oven temperature to 180°C/350°F/Gas 4. Cut the remaining pastry into strips and arrange them on top of the pie, gently teasing the strips into decorative loose swirls and folds, then brush the top of the pie with melted butter.

10 Bake the pie for 25–30 minutes more until the top is golden and crisp. Allow the pie to cool before transferring it to a large platter and serving.

Nutritional information per portion: Energy 468Kcal/1948kJ; Protein 10.7g; Carbohydrate 33g, of which sugars 3.5g; Fat 33.1g, of which saturates 20g; Cholesterol 137mg; Calcium 225mg; Fibre 3.2g; Sodium 218mg.

Sauerkraut stew with prunes

Dried fruits are often overlooked, but can be very exciting when used in vegetarian cuisine, not only for desserts but also to build subtle layers of flavour in main courses. In this dish, dried prunes have been used to add a subtle sweetness to the contrasting sour taste of the sauerkraut. Serve this wholesome stew as a main course with potatoes.

SERVES 4

700g/1lb 10oz sauerkraut

2 large onions

75–100g/3–3³⁄₄oz/6–7¹⁄₂ tbsp butter

5 black peppercorns

1 bay leaf

1 whole garlic bulb, about 10 cloves

200ml/7fl oz/scant 1 cup water

15ml/1 tbsp sugar

8 dried prunes

salt

1 Preheat the oven to 200°C/400°F/ Gas 6. Rinse the sauerkraut under running water if you find it too sour. Chop the onions. Heat the butter in a medium pan. Add the onions and fry for 5–8 minutes, stirring occasionally, until soft and golden brown. Add the sauerkraut and fork it through to mix with the fried onions and butter.

2 Add the peppercorns and bay leaf to the sauerkraut and onion mixture. Add the garlic bulb, without peeling or separating into cloves.

3 Transfer the sauerkraut mixture into an ovenproof dish. Add the water and sugar, and season with salt.

4 Bake the sauerkraut in the oven for 30 minutes, stirring occasionally. After 30 minutes, stir in the prunes. Return to the oven and bake for a further 20 minutes, stirring two or three times during cooking.

Nutritional information per portion: Energy 239kcal/986kJ; Protein 4.2g; Carbohydrate 21.2g, of which sugars 18.3g; Fat 15.7g, of which saturates 9.8g; Cholesterol 40mg; Calcium 142mg; Fibre 7g; Sodium 1298mg.

Courgette and potato bake

Cook this delicious dish in early autumn, and the aromas spilling from the kitchen will recall the rich summer tastes and colours just passed. It is especially mouthwatering when the potatoes on top are lightly scorched. This makes a truly satisfying main meal, accompanied by a salad, some olives and a selection of cheeses. It can be served hot or at room temperature.

SERVES 4

675g/1½lb courgettes (zucchini)
450g/1lb potatoes, peeled and cut
    into chunks
1 onion, finely sliced
3 garlic cloves, chopped
1 large red (bell) pepper, seeded
    and cubed
400g/14oz can chopped tomatoes
150ml/¼ pint/²/₃ cup extra virgin
    olive oil
150ml/¼ pint/²/₃ cup hot water
5ml/1 tsp dried oregano
45ml/3 tbsp chopped fresh flat
    leaf parsley
salt and ground black pepper

1 Preheat the oven to 190°C/375°F/Gas 5. Scrape the courgettes lightly under running water to dislodge any grit and then slice them into thin rounds. Put them in a large baking dish and add the potatoes, onion, garlic, red pepper and tomatoes. Mix well, then stir in the oil, hot water and oregano.

2 Spread the mixture evenly, then season with salt and pepper. Bake for 30 minutes, then stir in the parsley and a little more water.

3 Return the bake to the oven and cook for 1 hour more, increasing the oven temperature to 200°C/400°F/Gas 6 for the final 10–15 minutes, so that the potatoes brown.

Nutritional information per portion: Energy 374Kcal/1554kJ; Protein 6.6g; Carbohydrate 28.6g, of which sugars 11.2g; Fat 26.7g, of which saturates 4g; Cholesterol 0mg; Calcium 86mg; Fibre 5.1g; Sodium 29mg.

Vegetable stew with roasted tomato and garlic sauce

This lightly spiced stew makes a perfect match for couscous, enriched with butter. Add some fresh coriander, a handful of raisins and toasted pine nuts to the couscous to make it extra special.

SERVES 6

45ml/3 tbsp olive oil

250g/9oz small pickling (pearl) onions

1 large onion, chopped

2 garlic cloves, chopped

5ml/1 tsp cumin seeds

5ml/1 tsp ground coriander seeds

5ml/1 tsp paprika

5cm/2in piece cinnamon stick

2 fresh bay leaves

300–450ml/$\frac{1}{2}$–$\frac{3}{4}$ pint/$1\frac{1}{4}$–scant 2 cups
good vegetable stock

good pinch of saffron threads

450g/1lb carrots, thickly sliced

2 green (bell) peppers, seeded and thickly sliced

115g/4oz ready-to-eat dried apricots, halved
if large

5–7.5ml/1–1$\frac{1}{2}$ tsp ground toasted
cumin seeds

450g/1lb squash, peeled, seeded
and cut into chunks

pinch of sugar, to taste

25g/1oz/2 tbsp butter
(optional)

salt and ground black pepper

45ml/3 tbsp fresh coriander (cilantro)
leaves, to garnish

FOR THE ROASTED TOMATO AND GARLIC SAUCE

1kg/2$\frac{1}{4}$lb tomatoes, halved

5ml/1 tsp sugar

45ml/3 tbsp olive oil

1–2 fresh red chillies, seeded
and chopped

2–3 garlic cloves, chopped

5ml/1 tsp fresh thyme leaves

1 Preheat the oven to 180°C/350°F/Gas 4. First make the sauce. Place the tomatoes, cut sides uppermost, in a roasting pan. Season well with salt and pepper and sprinkle the sugar over the top, then drizzle with the olive oil. Roast for 30 minutes.

2 Scatter the chillies, garlic and thyme over the tomatoes, stir to mix and roast for another 30–45 minutes, until the tomatoes have collapsed but still a little juicy. Cool, then process in a food processor or blender to make a thick sauce. Sieve (strain) to remove the seeds.

3 Heat 30ml/2 tbsp of the oil in a large, wide pan or deep frying pan and cook the pickling onions until browned all over. Remove from the pan and set aside. Add the chopped onion to the pan and cook over a low heat for 5–7 minutes, until softened. Stir in the garlic and cumin seeds and cook for a further 3–4 minutes.

4 Add the ground coriander seeds, paprika, cinnamon stick and bay leaves. Cook, stirring constantly, for another 2 minutes, then mix in the vegetable stock, saffron, carrots and green peppers. Season well, cover and simmer gently for 10 minutes.

5 Stir in the apricots, 5ml/1 tsp of the ground toasted cumin seeds, the browned onions or shallots and the squash. Stir in the tomato sauce.

6 Cover the pan and cook for a further 5 minutes. Uncover the pan and continue to cook, stirring occasionally, for 10–15 minutes, until the vegetables are all fully cooked.

7 Adjust the seasoning, adding more cumin seeds and a pinch of sugar to taste. Remove and discard the cinnamon stick. Stir in the butter, if using, and serve sprinkled with the fresh coriander leaves.

Nutritional information per portion: Energy 166Kcal/690kJ; Protein 4.4g; Carbohydrate 18.3g, of which sugars 17.3g; Fat 8.8g, of which saturates 1.4g; Cholesterol 0mg; Calcium 6.8mg; Fibre 5.5g; Sodium 41mg.

Aubergines baked with tomatoes and cheese

This is a delectable dish, particularly when made in the middle of summer when the aubergines are at their sweetest. Perfect when served with salad for an alfresco meal.

SERVES 4

**4 large aubergines (eggplant), total
   weight about 1.2kg/2¹/₂lb**
150ml/¹/₄ pint /²/₃ cup sunflower oil
**50g/2oz/¹/₂ cup freshly grated Parmesan
   or Cheddar cheese**
salt and ground black pepper

FOR THE SAUCE
45ml/3 tbsp extra virgin olive oil
2 garlic cloves, crushed
2 x 400g/14oz cans tomatoes
5ml/1 tsp tomato purée (paste)
2.5ml/¹/₂ tsp sugar
2.5ml/¹/₂ tsp dried Greek oregano
**30–45ml/2–3 tbsp chopped fresh flat
   leaf parsley**

1 Preheat the oven to 180°C/350°F/ Gas 4. Trim the aubergines and cut lengthways into 1cm/¹/₂in thick slices.

2 Heat the oil in a large frying pan and fry the aubergine slices briefly in batches. Lift them out as soon as they are golden on both sides and drain them on kitchen paper.

3 Arrange the aubergine slices in two layers in a baking dish. Sprinkle with salt and pepper.

4 Make the sauce. Heat the oil gently in a large pan, add the garlic and sauté for a few seconds, then add the tomatoes, tomato purée, sugar and oregano and season. Cover and simmer for 25–30 minutes, until the sauce is velvety, stirring occasionally. Stir in the parsley and cook for 2–3 minutes.

5 Spread the tomato sauce over the aubergines to cover them completely. Sprinkle the cheese on top and bake for 40 minutes.

Nutritional information per portion: Energy 441kcal/1830kJ; Protein 9.4g; Carbohydrate 13.8g, of which sugars 13.2g; Fat 39.3g, of which saturates 7.7g; Cholesterol 13mg; Calcium 219mg; Fibre 8.6g; Sodium 165mg.

Onions with goat's cheese and sun-dried tomatoes

Roasted onions and goat's cheese are a winning combination. These stuffed onions make an excellent main course when served with a rice or cracked wheat pilaff.

SERVES 4

4 large onions

150g/5oz goat's cheese, crumbled
    or cubed

50g/2oz fresh breadcrumbs

8 sun-dried tomatoes in olive oil, drained
    and chopped

1–2 garlic cloves, finely chopped

2.5ml/½ tsp chopped fresh thyme

30ml/2 tbsp chopped fresh parsley

1 small egg, beaten

45ml/3 tbsp pine nuts, toasted

30ml/2 tbsp olive oil (use oil from
    the tomatoes)

salt and ground black pepper

1 Bring a large pan of lightly salted water to the boil. Add the whole onions in their skins and boil for 10 minutes. Drain and cool, then cut each onion in half horizontally and peel.

2 Using a teaspoon, remove the centre of each onion, leaving a thick shell. Reserve the flesh and place the shells in an oiled baking dish. Preheat the oven to 190°C/375°F/Gas 5.

3 Chop the scooped-out onion flesh and place in a bowl.

4 Add the goat's cheese, breadcrumbs, sun-dried tomatoes, garlic, thyme, parsley and egg to the chopped onion. Mix well, then season with salt and pepper and add the toasted pine nuts.

5 Divide the stuffing among the onion shells and cover with foil. Bake for about 25 minutes. Uncover, drizzle with the oil and cook for another 30–40 minutes, until bubbling and well cooked. Baste occasionally during cooking.

Nutritional information per portion: Energy 402Kcal/1669kJ; Protein 14.8g; Carbohydrate 25.1g, of which sugars 11.7g; Fat 27.7g, of which saturates 8.8g; Cholesterol 82mg; Calcium 120mg; Fibre 3.2g; Sodium 346mg.

Peppers filled with spiced vegetables

Indian spices season the potato and aubergine stuffing in these colourful baked peppers. They are delicious with plain rice and a lentil dhal. Alternatively, serve them with a salad, Indian breads and a flavoursome dip, such as a cucumber or mint and yogurt raita.

SERVES 6

6 large evenly shaped red or yellow
   (bell) peppers
500g/1¼lb waxy potatoes
1 small onion, chopped
4–5 garlic cloves, chopped
5cm/2in piece fresh root ginger, chopped
1–2 fresh green chillies, seeded and chopped
105ml/7 tbsp water
90–105ml/6–7 tbsp groundnut oil
1 aubergine (eggplant) , cut into 1cm/½in dice

10ml/2 tsp cumin seeds
5ml/1 tsp kalonji seeds
2.5ml/½ tsp ground turmeric
5ml/1 tsp ground coriander
5ml/1 tsp ground toasted cumin seeds
1-2 pinches of cayenne pepper
about 30ml/2 tbsp lemon juice
salt and ground black pepper
30ml/2 tbsp chopped fresh coriander
   (cilantro), to garnish

1 Cut the tops off the red or yellow peppers then remove and discard the seeds. Cut a thin slice off the base of the peppers, if necessary, to make them stand upright.

2 Bring a large pan of lightly salted water to the boil. Add the peppers and cook for 5–6 minutes. Drain and leave the peppers upside down in a colander to cool.

3 Cook the potatoes in boiling, salted water for 10–12 minutes, until just tender. Drain, cool and peel, then cut into 1cm/½in dice.

4 Put the onion, garlic, ginger and green chillies in a food processor or blender with 60ml/4 tbsp of the water and process to a purée.

5 Heat 45ml/3 tbsp of the oil in a large, deep frying pan and cook the aubergine, stirring occasionally, until browned on all sides. Remove from the pan and set aside. Add another 30ml/2 tbsp of the oil to the pan and cook the potatoes until lightly browned. Remove from the pan and set aside.

6 If necessary, add another 15ml/1 tbsp oil to the pan, then add the cumin and kalonji seeds. Fry briefly until the seeds darken, then add the turmeric, coriander and ground cumin. Cook for 15 seconds. Stir in the onion and garlic purée and fry, scraping the pan with a spatula, until it begins to brown.

7 Return the potatoes and aubergines to the pan, season with salt, pepper and 1–2 pinches of cayenne. Add the remaining water and 15ml/1 tbsp lemon juice and then cook, stirring, until the liquid evaporates. Preheat the oven to 190°C/375°F/Gas 5.

8 Fill the peppers with the potato mixture and place on a lightly greased baking tray. Brush the peppers with a little oil and bake for 30–35 minutes, until cooked. Allow to cool a little, then sprinkle with a little more lemon juice, garnish with the coriander and serve.

Nutritional information per portion: Energy 222Kcal/926kJ; Protein 3.6g; Carbohydrate 26.1g, of which sugars 13g; Fat 12.1g, of which saturates 2.5g; Cholesterol 0mg; Calcium 25mg; Fibre 4.4g; Sodium 17mg.

Fried mushrooms with root vegetables

Mushrooms soak up all of the flavours and juices that they are cooked in, and come in a variety of tastes and textures, so add variety to any meal. Here they are fried in butter and combined with a medley of root vegetables for a deliciously earthy and comforting result.

SERVES 4

350g/12oz fresh mushrooms, such as porcini, cut into small pieces
65g/2¹/₂oz/5 tbsp butter
2 onions, peeled and chopped
1 turnip, finely diced
3 carrots, finely diced
3–4 potatoes, finely diced
60–75ml/4–5 tbsp finely chopped fresh parsley
100ml/3¹/₂fl oz/scant ¹/₂ cup smetana or crème fraîche
salt and ground black pepper

1 Heat a large frying pan, add the mushrooms and cook over a medium heat, stirring frequently, until all liquid has evaporated. Add half of the butter and the onions to the pan and stir-fry for 10 minutes.

2 In a separate frying pan, melt the remaining butter. Add the turnip, carrots and potatoes, in two or three batches, and fry for 10–15 minutes, until softened and golden brown.

3 Mix the cooked mushrooms and the fried root vegetables together, cover the pan and cook over a gentle heat for about 10 minutes, until the vegetables are just tender. Season to taste.

4 Sprinkle the chopped parsley into the pan. Stir in the smetana or crème fraîche and reheat gently. Transfer the mixture to a warmed serving dish and serve hot.

Nutritional information per portion: Energy 361kcal/1503kJ; Protein 5.8g; Carbohydrate 31g, of which sugars 11.1g; Fat 24.7g, of which saturates 15.5g; Cholesterol 63mg; Calcium 94mg; Fibre 5.7g; Sodium 150mg.

Spinach gnocchi

These gnocchi are traditionally served simply with melted butter, but they can also be served with a basic tomato sauce. Don't worry about the uniformity of the dumplings, this is a rustic dish and part of its charm lies in the irregular shape of the gnocchi.

SERVES 6

1.3kg/3lb fresh spinach
2 eggs, beaten
2 egg yolks
30ml/2 tbsp single (light) cream
150g/5oz stale bread, soaked in milk to cover for 1/2 hour
150g/5oz/1 1/2 cups freshly grated Parmesan cheese
1.5ml/1/4 tsp freshly grated nutmeg
up to 75ml/5 tbsp plain (all-purpose) flour
115g/4oz unsalted butter, melted
sea salt and ground black pepper

1 Steam or boil the spinach for 1–2 minutes until soft. Drain and leave to cool. Squeeze out the water, then chop finely. Put the spinach in a large bowl and stir in the eggs and egg yolks, then the cream.

2 Squeeze the bread dry with your hands, then mix it into the spinach with half the Parmesan. Season to taste with nutmeg, salt and pepper. Bring a large pan of water to the boil.

3 Using your fingers and a very light touch, form the mixture into small dumplings, using a small amount of flour to prevent sticking.

4 Transfer the dumplings, in small batches, into boiling water. Cook for no more than 2–3 minutes – they will be ready when they float on the surface of the water.

5 Carefully remove the cooked gnocchi from the water using a slotted spoon and arrange them on a warmed serving dish. Continue with the remaining batches, until all the gnocchi are cooked.

6 Smother the gnocchi with the melted butter, sprinkle over the remaining Parmesan cheese and serve immediately.

Nutritional information per portion: Energy 465kcal/1933kJ; Protein 22.5g; Carbohydrate 25.7g, of which sugars 4.3g; Fat 30.8g, of which saturates 17.5g; Cholesterol 202mg; Calcium 738mg; Fibre 5.3g; Sodium 879mg.

Spinach and ricotta ravioli

Ricotta and spinach is a classic filling for ravioli. There are many variations on this recipe – other kinds of cheese can be added to the filling mixture, and instead of spinach, Swiss chard can be used.

SERVES 6

about 400g/14oz/3½ cups plain
　　(all-purpose) flour
50g/2oz/2 tbsp fine semolina, plus extra
　　for dusting
4 eggs
1 egg yolk
350g/12oz fresh ricotta cheese

500g/1¼lb spinach, cooked and
　　finely chopped
grated rind of 1 large unwaxed lemon
sea salt and ground black pepper
115g/4oz/1¼ cups freshly grated mild
　　Pecorino cheese, to garnish
tomato sauce or melted butter, to serve

1 Mix together the flour and semolina and place the mixture on a work surface in a mound. Use your fist to make a hollow in the centre.

2 Beat the eggs and egg yolk together and pour the mixture into the hollow in the flour. Work the flour and eggs together with your fingertips until you have a pliable ball of dough that is neither too sticky or too dry – add more flour if required.

3 Knead the ball of dough until it is smooth and elastic. Cover with a clean cloth or wrap in clear film (plastic wrap), and leave to rest for about 30 minutes while you make the filling for the ravioli.

4 In a large bowl, mix together the ricotta cheese, chopped spinach and grated lemon rind. Season to taste with salt and pepper.

5 Roll out the dough into a long, thin rectangle as finely and as evenly as possible. Drop the filling, in a neat row, along half the sheet of dough, a scant tablespoon at a time, leaving about 2.5cm/1in between the little mounds of filling. Fold the sheet over to cover the filling.

6 With your fingers, press down firmly between the mounds of filling so that the dough sticks together and closes up like a little parcel. Cut out the ravioli with a serrated pasta cutter or knife and press round the edges again to make sure each is perfectly sealed.

7 Dust a wide baking tray with semolina and lay the ravioli over it, taking care not to overlap them or lay them on top of one another.

8 Bring a large pan of water to the boil and drop in the ravioli. Cook for 3–4 minutes, in batches. They should rise to the surface when cooked. Scoop out the ravioli using a large slotted spoon as soon as they are cooked, and transfer them to a warmed bowl.

9 Dress the ravioli with tomato sauce or melted butter and sprinkle with freshly grated mild Pecorino cheese.

Nutritional information per portion: Energy 513kcal/2155kJ; Protein 26.3g; Carbohydrate 61.2g, of which sugars 3.8g; Fat 19.8g, of which saturates 10g; Cholesterol 201mg; Calcium 489mg; Fibre 4g; Sodium 377mg.

Spaghetti with wild asparagus

The secret of this recipe is in the simplicity of just a few carefully-selected ingredients. Wild asparagus is famous for its amazingly bright green colour and its intense flavour. Good-quality, store-bought asparagus, or sprue, which are the first pickings and have thinner stems, can be used in the place of the wild asparagus.

SERVES 6

60ml/4 tbsp olive oil

2 garlic cloves, peeled and left whole

900g/2lb fresh wild asparagus, fine local asparagus or sprue, cut into short sections

450g/1lb ripe tomatoes, peeled, seeded and chopped

450g/1lb spaghetti

sea salt and ground black pepper

freshly grated Parmesan cheese, to serve

1 Heat the olive oil in a pan and fry the garlic gently until golden brown. Discard the garlic. Add the asparagus to the garlic-flavoured oil. Stir and cook gently for about 5 minutes, until tender.

2 Add the tomatoes to the asparagus and stir together. Season to taste.

3 Cook the spaghetti in a large pan of salted boiling water, until al dente. Drain and return to the pan.

4 Pour the asparagus sauce over the pasta and mix together gently.

5 Transfer to a warm serving dish and serve immediately, with the Parmesan cheese offered separately.

Nutritional information per portion: Energy 373kcal/1572kJ; Protein 13.9g; Carbohydrate 60.9g, of which sugars 7.7g; Fat 9.8g, of which saturates 1.4g; Cholesterol 0mg; Calcium 65mg; Fibre 5.5g; Sodium 11mg.

Pasta and chickpeas

This simple, thick pasta stew is intended to be a satisfying, cheap, nourishing and tasty meal that relies on the addition of other available ingredients to enrich and improve on the basic recipe. You could easily add other vegetables, such as shredded cabbage, ripe tomatoes or chopped courgettes, towards the end of cooking.

SERVES 6

1kg/2¼lb dried chickpeas, soaked overnight and drained
2 celery sticks
2 carrots
2 onions, peeled and halved
4 garlic cloves
2 x 15cm/6in sprigs fresh rosemary
450g/1lb short ribbed pasta, such as ditalini
sea salt and ground black pepper
extra virgin olive oil, to serve

1 Rinse the drained chickpeas. Put them in a large pan and cover with plenty of water. Bring to the boil and boil hard for 5 minutes, then drain and rinse again.

2 Return the chickpeas to the pan, cover with fresh water and add the vegetables and rosemary sprigs. Bring to the boil and simmer gently for 45 minutes. Remove and discard the vegetables.

3 Blend one-third of the chickpeas in a blender or food processor until smooth, then return to the pan. Stir, season and simmer for 20 minutes.

4 Cook the pasta in a pan of salted boiling water until almost tender. Drain the pasta, stir it into the chickpeas, then boil everything for about a minute, stirring gently. Adjust the seasoning, and serve. Offer olive oil to diners to drizzle over their stew.

Nutritional information per portion: Energy 820kcal/3477kJ; Protein 45.4g; Carbohydrate 144.9g, of which sugars 12.2g; Fat 10.6g, of which saturates 1g; Cholesterol 0mg; Calcium 310mg; Fibre 21.6g; Sodium 83mg.

Vegetable and marinated tofu pasta

This recipe is very versatile. Feel inspired to change it to suit the ingredients you have to hand. Chop all the vegetables into even-size pieces so that they all cook by the same time.

SERVES 4

4 carrots, halved lengthways and thinly
    sliced diagonally
1 butternut squash, peeled, seeded and
    cut into small chunks
2 courgettes (zucchini), sliced diagonally
1 red onion, cut into wedges
1 red (bell) pepper, sliced into thick strips
1 garlic bulb, cut in half horizontally
60ml/4 tbsp olive oil
60ml/4 tbsp balsamic vinegar
30ml/2 tbsp soy sauce
500g/1¼lb marinated deep-fried tofu
10–12 cherry tomatoes, halved
250g/9oz dried pasta, such fusilli or penne
sea salt and ground black pepper

1 Preheat the oven to 220°C/425°F/ Gas 7. Arrange the carrots, butternut squash, courgettes, onion wedges and pepper in a roasting pan.

2 Add the garlic, then drizzle over the olive oil, balsamic vinegar and soy sauce. Season then mix together to coat with the oil.

3 Roast for 50–60 minutes, until lightly browned at the edges. Toss the vegetables once or twice during cooking to ensure even cooking.

4 Add the tofu and tomatoes to the roasting pan 10 minutes before the end of cooking. Bring a pan of salted water to the boil, add the pasta and cook for until al dente. Drain the pasta and return to the pan with a few tablespoons of the cooking water.

5 Remove the roasting pan from the oven and squeeze the garlic out its skin using a spoon. Toss the pasta with the vegetables and tofu, and adjust the seasoning, if necessary. Serve immediately.

Nutritional information per portion: Energy 719Kcal/3009kJ; Protein 41.2g; Carbohydrate 63.4g, of which sugars 15.4g; Fat 35.1g, of which saturates 2g; Cholesterol 0mg; Calcium 1958mg; Fibre 6.6g; Sodium 464mg.

Tofu balls with spaghetti

This dish makes a great family supper, as children and adults alike love the little tofu balls and the rich vegetable sauce, while pasta never fails to please.

SERVES 4

250g/9oz firm tofu, drained
1 onion, coarsely grated
2 garlic cloves, crushed
5ml/1 tsp Dijon mustard
1 small bunch of parsley, finely chopped
50g/2oz/1/2 cup ground almonds
30ml/2 tbsp olive oil
350g/12oz spaghetti

FOR THE SAUCE
15ml/1 tbsp olive oil
1 large onion, finely chopped
2 garlic cloves, chopped
1 large aubergine (eggplant), diced
2 courgettes (zucchini), diced
400g/14oz can chopped tomatoes
200ml/7fl oz/scant 1 cup vegetable stock
1 bunch of fresh basil
salt and ground black pepper

1 Place the tofu, onion, garlic, mustard, parsley and almonds into a bowl and mix thoroughly. Roll into about 20 walnut-sized balls, squashing the mixture together with your hands.

2 Heat the olive oil in a frying pan, then cook the balls, turning them gently until brown all over. Remove from the pan and set aside on a plate.

3 To make the sauce, heat the oil in the same pan, add the onion and garlic and cook for 5 minutes, until soft.

4 Add the aubergine, courgette and seasoning and stir-fry for 10 minutes until the vegetables are beginning to soften.

5 Stir in the tomatoes and stock. Cover and simmer for 20–30 minutes, until the sauce is rich and thick. Place the tofu balls on top of the sauce, replace the lid and cook for 3 minutes.

6 Cook the pasta in pan of salted, boiling water, then drain. Sprinkle the sauce with the basil and serve with the spaghetti.

Nutritional information per portion: Energy 576Kcal/2422kJ; Protein 22.5g; Carbohydrate 79.4g, of which sugars 15.6g; Fat 21g, of which saturates 2.6g; Cholesterol 0mg; Calcium 165mg; Fibre 14.9g; Sodium 689mg.

Mushroom polenta

This recipe uses freshly made polenta, but for an even easier version you can substitute ready-made polenta and slice it straight into the dish, ready for baking. The cheesy mushroom topping is also delicious on toasted herb or sun-dried tomato bread as a light lunch or supper. Any combination of mushrooms will work – try a mixture of button (white) and wild mushrooms as an alternative.

SERVES FOUR

250g/9oz/1¹/₂ cups quick-cook polenta
50g/2oz/¹/₄ cup butter
400g/14oz chestnut mushrooms, sliced
175g/6oz/1¹/₂ cups grated
   Gruyère cheese
salt and ground black pepper

1 Line a 28 x 18cm/11 x 7in shallow baking tin (pan) with baking parchment. Bring 1 litre/1³/₄ pints/4 cups water with 5ml/1 tsp salt to the boil in a large pan. Add the polenta in a steady stream, stirring constantly. Bring back to the boil, stirring, and cook for 5 minutes, until thick and smooth. Transfer the polenta to the prepared tin and spread it out into an even layer. Leave to cool.

2 Preheat the oven to 200°C/400°F/Gas 6. Melt the butter in a frying pan and cook the mushrooms for 3–5 minutes, until golden. Season with salt and lots of freshly ground black pepper.

3 Turn out the polenta on to a chopping board. Peel away the parchment and cut the polenta into large squares. Pile the squares into a shallow, ovenproof dish. Sprinkle with half the cheese, then pile the mushrooms on top and pour over their buttery juices. Sprinkle with the remaining cheese and bake for about 20 minutes, until the cheese is melting and pale golden.

Nutritional information per portion: Energy 518Kcal/2155kJ; Protein 18.9g; Carbohydrate 46.2g, of which sugars 0.3g; Fat 27.2g, of which saturates 16.1g; Cholesterol 69mg; Calcium 334mg; Fibre 2.5g; Sodium 397mg.

Mushroom stroganoff

This creamy mushroom sauce is ideal for a dinner party. Serve it with toasted buckwheat, brown rice or a mixture of wild rices, and garnish with chopped chives. For best results, choose a variety of different mushrooms – wild mushrooms such as chanterelles, ceps and morels add a delicious flavour and texture to the stroganoff, as well as adding colour and producing a decorative appearance.

SERVES FOUR

25g/1oz/2 tbsp butter

900g/2lb mixed mushrooms, cut into
    bitesize pieces, including $2/3$ button
    (white) mushrooms and $1/3$ assorted
    wild or exotic mushrooms

350ml/12fl oz/1$1/2$ cups white
    wine sauce

250ml/8fl oz/1 cup sour cream

1 Melt the butter in a pan and quickly cook the mushrooms, in batches, over a high heat, until brown. Transfer the mushrooms to a bowl after cooking each batch.

2 Add the sauce to the juices remaining in the pan and bring to the boil, stirring. Reduce the heat and replace the mushrooms with any juices from the bowl. Stir well and heat for a few seconds, then remove from the heat.

3 Stir the sour cream into the cooked mushroom mixture and season to taste with salt and lots of freshly ground black pepper. Heat through gently for a few seconds, if necessary, then transfer to warm plates and serve immediately.

Nutritional information per portion: Energy 408Kcal/1685kJ; Protein 6.5g; Carbohydrate 14.3g, of which sugars 6.3g; Fat 34.4g, of which saturates 22.4g; Cholesterol 92mg; Calcium 81mg; Fibre 3.4g; Sodium 88mg.

Smoked aubergines in cheese sauce

This recipe is from Turkey, where it was originally created for one of the Ottoman sultans. It is a warming and nourishing dish that is popular with children. Serve it as a main dish for lunch or supper with chunks of fresh, crusty bread and a refreshing green salad.

SERVES 4

2 large aubergines (eggplants)
50g/2oz/¼ cup butter
30ml/2 tbsp plain (all-purpose) flour
600ml/1 pint/2½ cups milk, plus extra
    if needed

115g/4oz Cheddar cheese,
    grated
salt and ground black pepper
finely grated Parmesan cheese,
    for the topping

1 Preheat the oven to 200°C/400°F/ Gas 6. Put the aubergines directly on the gas flame on top of the stove, or under a conventional grill (broiler), and turn them until the skin is charred on all sides and the flesh feels soft. Place in a plastic bag and leave for a few minutes.

2 Hold each aubergine by the stalk under cold running water and gently peel off the charred skin.

3 Squeeze the flesh with your fingers to get rid of any excess water and place on a chopping board. Remove the stalks and chop the flesh to a pulp.

4 Make the sauce. Melt the butter in a heavy pan, remove from the heat and stir in the flour. Slowly beat in the milk, then return the pan to a medium heat and cook, stirring constantly, until the sauce is smooth and thick.

5 Beat in the grated Cheddar cheese a little at a time, then beat in the aubergine pulp and season with salt and pepper.

6 Transfer the mixture to a baking dish and sprinkle a generous layer of Parmesan over the top.

7 Bake in the oven for about 25 minutes, until the top is nicely browned.

Nutritional information per portion: Energy 322kcal/1344kJ; Protein 14.1g; Carbohydrate 15.2g, of which sugars 9.3g; Fat 22.7g, of which saturates 14.5g; Cholesterol 63mg; Calcium 415mg; Fibre 2.2g; Sodium 350mg.

Mixed-bean chilli with cornbread topping

Gently cooked in a slow cooker, this recipe combines chilli with Texan cornbread. The delicious topping offers the starch component of the dish, making this dish a filling meal.

SERVES 4

115g/4oz/ ½ cup dried red kidney beans
115g/4oz/½ cup dried black-eyed beans
600ml/1 pint/2½ cups cold water
1 bay leaf
15ml/1 tbsp vegetable oil
1 large onion, finely chopped
1 garlic clove, crushed
5ml/1 tsp ground cumin
5ml/1 tsp chilli powder
5ml/1 tsp mild paprika
2.5ml/½ tsp dried marjoram
450g/1lb mixed vegetables, such as
    potatoes, carrots, aubergines
    (eggplants), parsnips and celery
1 vegetable stock cube
400g/14oz can chopped tomatoes
15ml/1 tbsp tomato purée (paste)
salt and ground black pepper

FOR THE CORNBREAD TOPPING

250g/9oz/2¼ cups fine cornmeal
30ml/2 tbsp wholemeal
    (whole-wheat) flour
7.5ml/1½ tsp baking powder
1 egg, plus 1 egg yolk, lightly beaten
300ml/½ pint/1¼ cups milk

1 Put the dried beans in a large bowl with plenty of cold water, to cover. Leave to soak for at least 6 hours.

2 Drain and rinse the beans, then place in a pan with the cold water and the bay leaf. Bring to the boil and boil rapidly for 10 minutes. Leave to cool for a few minutes, then transfer to a slow cooker pot and switch to high.

3 Heat the oil in a pan, add the onion and cook for 7–8 minutes. Add the garlic, cumin, chilli powder, paprika and marjoram and cook for 1 minute. Transfer to the pot and stir.

4 Gather the vegetables, then cut into 2cm/¾in chunks. Add to the pot, cover and cook for 3 hours.

5 Stir the stock cube, tomatoes and tomato purée into the pot and season. Cover and cook for about 30 minutes until the mixture is at boiling point. Discard the bay leaf.

6 To make the topping, combine the cornmeal, flour, baking powder and a pinch of salt. Make a well in the centre and add the egg, egg yolk and milk. Mix, then spoon over the bean mixture. Cover and cook for 1 hour, or until firm.

Nutritional information per portion: Energy 613Kcal/2595kJ; Protein 29.6g; Carbohydrate 97.4g, of which sugars 15.8g; Fat 14.5g, of which saturates 3.4g; Cholesterol 112mg; Calcium 257mg; Fibre 13.4g; Sodium 413mg.

Tagine of butter beans, cherry tomatoes and olives

This hearty dish is substantial enough to be served as a main dish, with a leafy salad and fresh, crusty bread. If you are in a hurry, you could use two 400g/14oz cans of butter beans for this tagine.

SERVES 4

115g/4oz/²⁄₃ cup butter (lima) beans, soaked overnight

30–45ml/2–3 tbsp olive oil

1 onion, chopped

2–3 garlic cloves, crushed

25g/1oz fresh root ginger, peeled and chopped

pinch of saffron threads

16 cherry tomatoes

generous pinch of sugar

handful of fleshy black olives, pitted

5ml/1 tsp ground cinnamon

5ml/1 tsp paprika

small bunch of flat leaf parsley, chopped, to garnish

salt and ground black pepper

1 Rinse and drain the beans, and place them in a large pan with plenty of water. Bring to the boil and boil for about 10 minutes, then reduce the heat and simmer gently for 1–1½ hours until tender. Drain the beans and refresh under cold water.

2 Heat the olive oil in a heavy pan. Add the onion, garlic and ginger, and cook for about 10 minutes, until soft.

3 Stir the saffron threads into the pan, followed by the cherry tomatoes and a pinch of sugar.

4 As the tomatoes begin to soften, stir in the butter beans. When the tomatoes have heated through, stir in the olives, ground cinnamon and paprika. Season to taste and sprinkle over the parsley. Serve the tagine immediately.

Nutritional information per portion: Energy 117Kcal/487kJ; Protein 3.5g; Carbohydrate 8.5g, of which sugars 2.2g; Fat 7.9g, of which saturates 1.2g; Cholesterol 0mg; Calcium 25mg; Fibre 3.3g; Sodium 635mg.

Tagine of yam, carrots and prunes

The vegetables in this succulent, syrupy tagine should be slightly caramelized. They are at their best served with couscous or with warm, crusty bread and a leafy, herb-filled salad. You can also make this wonderfully moreish dish with sweet potatoes if yams are difficult to find.

SERVES 4–6

45ml/3 tbsp olive oil

a little butter

25–30 pickling or button (pearl) onions, blanched and peeled

900g/2lb yam or sweet potatoes, peeled and cut into bitesize chunks

2–3 carrots, cut into bitesize chunks

150g/5oz/generous ¹/₂ cup ready-to-eat pitted prunes

5ml/1 tsp ground cinnamon

2.5ml/¹/₂ tsp ground ginger

10ml/2 tsp clear honey

450ml/³/₄ pint/scant 2 cups vegetable stock

small bunch of fresh coriander (cilantro), finely chopped

small bunch of mint, finely chopped

salt and ground black pepper

1 Preheat the oven to 200°C/400°F/Gas 6. Heat the olive oil in a flameproof casserole with the butter and stir in the peeled onions. Cook for about 5 minutes until the onions are tender, then remove half of the onions from the pan and set aside.

2 Add the yam or sweet potatoes and carrots to the pan and cook until lightly browned. Stir in the prunes with the cinnamon, ginger and honey, then pour in the stock. Season well, cover the casserole and transfer to the oven for about 45 minutes.

3 Stir in the reserved onions and bake for a further 10 minutes. Gently stir in the fresh coriander and mint, and serve the tagine immediately.

Nutritional information per portion: Energy 388Kcal/1638kJ; Protein 5.4g; Carbohydrate 74.8g, of which sugars 37.5g; Fat 9.6g, of which saturates 1.5g; Cholesterol 0mg; Calcium 129mg; Fibre 11g; Sodium 120mg.

Tagine of artichoke hearts, potatoes and saffron

Fresh coriander, parsley and mint combine here to complement the summery flavours of the vegetables, while turmeric contributes its earthy warmth. Prepare the artichokes yourself by removing the outer leaves, cutting off the stems, and scooping out the hairy choke with a teaspoon, or, as an alternative, buy frozen prepared hearts.

SERVES 4–6

6 fresh artichoke hearts
juice of 1 lemon
30–45ml/2–3 tbsp olive oil
1 onion, chopped
675g/1½lb potatoes, peeled
   and quartered
small bunch of flat leaf parsley, chopped
small bunch of coriander (cilantro), chopped
small bunch of mint, chopped
pinch of saffron threads
5ml/1 tsp ground turmeric
350ml/12fl oz/1½ cups vegetable stock
finely chopped rind of ½ preserved lemon
250g/9oz/2¼ cups shelled peas
salt and ground black pepper
couscous or bread, to serve

1 Poach the artichokes in plenty of simmering water with half the lemon juice, for 10–15 minutes. Drain and refresh under cold running water.

2 Heat the olive oil in a tagine or heavy pan. Add the chopped onion and cook over a low heat for about 15 minutes, or until softened but not browned. Add the potatoes, most of the parsley, the coriander, mint, the remaining lemon juice, and the saffron and turmeric to the pan. Pour in the vegetable stock, bring to the boil, then reduce the heat. Cover the pan and cook for about 15 minutes, or until the potatoes are almost tender.

3 Stir the preserved lemon, artichoke hearts and peas into the stew, and cook, uncovered, for a further 10 minutes. Season to taste, sprinkle with the remaining parsley, and serve with couscous or chunks of fresh bread.

Nutritional information per portion: Energy 141Kcal/591kJ; Protein 3g; Carbohydrate 19.5g, of which sugars 2.4g; Fat 6.2g, of which saturates 0.9g; Cholesterol 0mg; Calcium 62mg; Fibre 2.7g; Sodium 48mg.

Butternut squash with caramelized pink shallots

You can serve this as a meal on its own, as an accompaniment, or as a topping for couscous.
A dollop of garlic-flavoured yogurt or a spoonful of harissa goes very well with this dish.

SERVES 4

900g/2lb peeled butternut squash, cut into thick slices
120ml/4fl oz/¹/₂ cup water
45–60ml/3–4 tbsp olive oil
knob (pat) of butter
16–20 pink shallots, peeled
10–12 garlic cloves, peeled
115g/4oz/1 cup blanched almonds
75g/3oz/generous ¹/₂ cup raisins or sultanas (golden raisins), soaked in warm water for 15 minutes and drained
30–45ml/2–3 tbsp clear honey
10ml/2 tsp ground cinnamon
salt and ground black pepper
chopped mint, to garnish (optional)
lemon wedges, to serve (optional)

1 Preheat the oven to 200°C/400°F/Gas 6. Place the butternut squash in an ovenproof dish, add the water, cover and bake for about 45 minutes, until tender.

2 Meanwhile, heat the olive oil and butter in a large heavy pan. Stir in the shallots and cook until they begin to brown. Stir in the garlic and almonds. When the garlic and almonds begin to brown, add the raisins or sultanas.

3 Continue to cook until the shallots and garlic begin to caramelize, then stir in the honey and cinnamon, adding a little water if the mixture is too dry. Season well with salt and pepper and remove from the heat.

4 Cover the squash with the shallot and garlic mixture and return to the oven, uncovered, for a further 15 minutes. Sprinkle with fresh mint and serve with lemon wedges, if you like.

Nutritional information per portion: Energy 395kcal/1648kJ; Protein 9.3g; Carbohydrate 35.5g, of which sugars 31.3g; Fat 25g, of which saturates 2.7g; Cholesterol 0mg; Calcium 169mg; Fibre 6.2g; Sodium 20mg.

Summer vegetable kebabs with yogurt dip

This tasty dish is delicious served with couscous and a fresh salad. Vegetable kebabs are very adaptable and can also be cooked on the barbecue.

SERVES 4

2 aubergines (eggplant), part peeled and
    cut into chunks
2 courgettes (zucchini), cut into chunks
2–3 red (bell) peppers, cut into chunks
12–16 cherry tomatoes
4 small red onions, quartered
60ml/4 tbsp olive oil
juice of ½ lemon
1 garlic clove, crushed
5ml/1 tsp ground coriander
5ml/1 tsp ground cinnamon
10ml/2 tsp clear honey
5ml/1 tsp salt

FOR THE DIP
450g/1lb/2 cups Greek (US strained
    plain) yogurt
30–60ml/2–4 tbsp harissa
bunch of fresh coriander (cilantro), chopped
small bunch of mint, chopped
salt and ground black pepper

1 Preheat the grill (broiler) on the hottest setting. Put all the vegetables in a bowl. Mix the olive oil, lemon juice, garlic, ground coriander, cinnamon, honey and salt and pour the mixture over the vegetables.

2 Toss the vegetables gently in the marinade, then thread them on to metal skewers.

3 Cook the kebabs under the grill, turning them occasionally until the vegetables are nicely browned all over.

4 To make the dip, put the yogurt in a bowl and beat in the harissa, making it as fiery as you like by adding more. Add most of the chopped coriander and mint, reserving a little to use as a garnish, and season to taste with salt and pepper.

5 While they are still hot, slide the cooked vegetables off the skewers and dunk them into the yogurt dip before eating. Garnish the yogurt-coated kebabs with the reserved herbs.

Nutritional information per portion: Energy 305Kcal/1267kJ; Protein 9.9g; Carbohydrate 24.8g, of which sugars 22.6g; Fat 19.1g, of which saturates 6.6g; Cholesterol 16mg; Calcium 230mg; Fibre 5.2g; Sodium 181mg.

Jewelled vegetable rice with crispy eggs

Inspired by the traditional Indonesian dish nasi goreng, this vibrant, colourful stir-fry makes a tasty light meal. To make an extra-nutritious option, use brown basmati rice in place of white.

SERVES 4

30ml/2 tbsp sunflower oil
2 garlic cloves, finely chopped
4 red Asian shallots, thinly sliced
1 small red chilli, finely sliced
90g/3¹⁄₂oz carrots, cut into matchsticks
90g/3¹⁄₂oz fine green beans, cut into
   2cm/³⁄₄in lengths
90g/3¹⁄₂oz fresh corn
1 red (bell) pepper, seeded and cut into
   1cm/¹⁄₂in dice
90g/3¹⁄₂oz button (white) mushrooms
500g/1¹⁄₄lb cooked, cooled long grain rice
45ml/3 tbsp light soy sauce
10ml/2 tsp vegetarian green curry paste
4 crispy fried eggs, to serve
crisp green salad leaves and lime wedges,
   to serve

1 Heat the sunflower oil in a wok over a high heat. When hot, add the garlic, shallots and chilli. Stir-fry for about 2 minutes.

2 Add the carrots, green beans, corn, red pepper and mushrooms to the wok and stir-fry for 3–4 minutes. Add the cooked, cooled rice and stir-fry for a further 4–5 minutes.

3 Mix together the light soy sauce and curry paste and add to the wok. Toss to mix in well with the rice and vegetables and stir-fry for around 2–3 minutes until hot.

4 Ladle the rice into four bowls and top each portion with a fried egg. Serve with crisp salad leaves and wedges of lime to squeeze over.

Nutritional information per portion: Energy 474Kcal/1979kJ; Protein 22.5g; Carbohydrate 77.5g, of which sugars 4.3g; Fat 7.8g, of which saturates 1.1g; Cholesterol 48mg; Calcium 86mg; Fibre 1.9g; Sodium 710mg.

Barley risotto with roasted squash and leeks

This is more like a pilaff, made with slightly chewy, nutty-flavoured pearl barley, than a classic risotto. Sweet leeks and roasted squash are superb with this earthy grain.

SERVES 4–5

200g/7oz/1 cup pearl barley

1 butternut squash, peeled, seeded and
   cut into chunks

10ml/2 tsp chopped fresh thyme

60ml/4 tbsp olive oil

25g/1oz/2 tbsp butter

4 leeks, cut into fairly thick diagonal slices

2 garlic cloves, finely chopped

175g/6oz chestnut mushrooms, sliced

2 carrots, coarsely grated

about 120ml/4fl oz/¹/₂ cup vegetable
   stock

30ml/2 tbsp chopped fresh flat
   leaf parsley

50g/2oz Pecorino cheese, grated
   or shaved

salt and ground black pepper

45ml/3 tbsp pumpkin seeds, toasted,
   to garnish

1 Rinse the barley, then cook it in simmering water, keeping the pan part-covered, for 35–45 minutes, or until tender. Drain. Preheat the oven to 200°C/400°F/Gas 6.

2 Place the squash in a roasting pan with half the thyme. Season with pepper and toss with half the oil. Roast, stirring the squash once, for 30–35 minutes, until tender and beginning to brown.

3 Heat half the butter with the remaining oil in a frying pan. Cook the leeks and garlic gently for 5 minutes.

4 Add the mushrooms and remaining thyme, then cook until the liquid from the mushrooms evaporates and they begin to fry.

5 Stir in the carrots and cook for 2 minutes, then add the barley and most of the stock. Season well and part-cover the pan. Cook for a further 5 minutes. Pour in the remaining stock if the mixture seems too dry.

6 Stir in the parsley, the remaining butter and half the Pecorino. Then stir in the squash. Season and serve, sprinkled with the toasted pumpkin seeds and the remaining Pecorino.

Nutritional information per portion: Energy 498Kcal/2089kJ; Protein 15.6g; Carbohydrate 55.6g, of which sugars 11.2g; Fat 25.2g, of which saturates 5.2g; Cholesterol 13mg; Calcium 287mg; Fibre 7.6g; Sodium 156mg.

Pumpkin, rosemary and chilli risotto

A dangerously rich and creamy risotto. The pumpkin gradually disintegrates to speckle the rice with orange. The rosemary gives it a sweet pungency, while garlic and chilli add bite.

SERVES 4

115g/4oz/¹/₂ cup butter

1 small onion, finely chopped

2 large garlic cloves, crushed

1 fresh red chilli, seeded and
finely chopped

250g/9oz fresh pumpkin or butternut
squash, peeled and roughly chopped

30ml/2 tbsp chopped fresh rosemary

250g/9oz/1¹/₂ cups risotto rice,
preferably Arborio or Vialone Nano

about 750ml/1¹/₄ pints/3 cups hot
vegetable stock, preferably fresh

50g/2oz/²/₃ cup freshly grated Parmesan
cheese, plus extra to serve

salt and ground black pepper

1 Melt half the butter in a pan, add the onion and garlic, and cook for 10 minutes until soft. Add the chilli and cook for 1 minute. Add the pumpkin or squash and cook for 5 minutes. Stir in the rosemary.

2 Add the rice, and stir with a wooden spoon to coat with the oil and vegetables. Cook for 2–3 minutes to toast the rice grains.

3 Begin to add the stock, stirring in a ladleful at a time until it has been absorbed into the rice. The rice should always be bubbling slowly.

4 Continue adding the stock like this, until the rice is tender and creamy, but the grains remain firm, and the pumpkin is beginning to disintegrate. (This should take about 20 minutes, depending on the type of rice used.) Taste and season well with salt and pepper.

5 Stir the remaining butter and the Parmesan cheese into the rice. Cover and let the risotto rest for 2–3 minutes.

6 Serve the risotto straight away with extra Parmesan cheese.

Nutritional information per portion: Energy 585Kcal/2441kJ; Protein 14.4g; Carbohydrate 87.3g, of which sugars 5.7g; Fat 15.9g, of which saturates 3.5g; Cholesterol 8mg; Calcium 196mg; Fibre 3.2g; Sodium 151mg.

Potato curry with yogurt

This simple Indian curry is delicious on its own, served with yogurt and a spicy pickle or chutney. A dry version, without yogurt, can be used to fill tasty flatbreads and savoury pastries.

SERVES 4

6 garlic cloves, chopped

25g/1oz root ginger, peeled and chopped

30ml/2 tbsp ghee

6 shallots, halved lengthways and sliced

2 green chillies, seeded and finely sliced

10ml/2 tsp sugar

a handful of fresh or dried curry leaves

2 cinnamon sticks

5–10ml/1–2 tsp ground turmeric

15ml/1 tbsp garam masala

500g/1¼lb waxy potatoes, diced

2 tomatoes, peeled, seeded and quartered

250ml/8fl oz/1 cup Greek (US strained plain) yogurt

salt and ground black pepper

5ml/1 tsp red chilli powder, and fresh coriander (cilantro) and mint leaves, finely chopped, to garnish

1 lemon, quartered, to serve

1 Using a mortar and pestle or a food processor, grind the garlic and ginger to a coarse paste.

2 Heat the ghee in a pan and stir in the shallots and chillies, until fragrant. Add the garlic and ginger paste with the sugar, and stir until the mixture begins to colour.

3 Stir in the curry leaves, cinnamon sticks, turmeric and garam masala, and toss in the potatoes, making sure they are well coated in the spice mixture.

4 Pour in enough cold water to cover the potatoes. Bring to the boil, then reduce to a simmer until the potatoes are just cooked – they should still have a bite to them.

5 Season with salt and pepper to taste. Gently toss in the tomatoes to heat them through. Fold in the yogurt so that it is streaky rather than completely mixed in. Sprinkle with the chilli powder, coriander and mint. Serve immediately from the pan, with lemon to squeeze over it and flatbread for scooping it up.

Nutritional information per portion: Energy 231Kcal/967kJ; Protein 6.7g; Carbohydrate 26.2g, of which sugars 7.4g; Fat 12.4g, of which saturates 4.1g; Cholesterol 0mg; Calcium 110mg; Fibre 2g; Sodium 63mg.

Pineapple and coconut curry

This sweet and spicy curry benefits from being made the day before eating, enabling the flavours to mingle longer. Traditionally it is eaten at room temperature, but it is also delicious hot.

SERVES 4

1 small, firm pineapple
155–30ml/1–2 tbsp palm or coconut oil
4–6 shallots, finely chopped
2 garlic cloves, finely chopped
1 red chilli, seeded and finely chopped
15ml/1 tbsp palm sugar (jaggery)
400ml/14fl oz/1²/₃ cups coconut milk
salt and ground black pepper
1 small bunch fresh coriander (cilantro)
    leaves, to garnish

FOR THE SPICE PASTE

4 cloves
4 cardamom pods
1 small cinnamon stick
5ml/1 tsp coriander seeds
2.5ml/1/2 tsp cumin seeds
5–10ml/1–2 tsp water

1 Make the spice paste. Using a mortar and pestle grind all the spices together. Mix the spice powder with the water to make a paste. Put aside.

2 Skin the pineapple then cut the flesh lengthways into quarters and remove the core. Cut each quarter widthways into slices and put aside.

3 Heat the oil in a wok, stir in the shallots, garlic and chilli and stir-fry until fragrant and beginning to colour. Stir in the spice paste and fry for 1 minute. Toss in the pineapple, making sure the slices are coated in the spicy mixture.

4 Stir the sugar into the coconut milk and pour into the wok. Stir and bring to the boil. Reduce the heat and simmer for 3–4 minutes to thicken the sauce, but do not allow the pineapple to become too soft. Season to taste.

5 Transfer the curry to a warmed serving dish and sprinkle with the coriander leaves to garnish. Serve hot or at room temperature.

Nutritional information per portion: Energy 135kcal/573kJ; Protein 1.6g; Carbohydrate 25.4g, of which sugars 23.6g; Fat 3.8g, of which saturates 0.5g; Cholesterol 0mg; Calcium 87mg; Fibre 2.9g; Sodium 131mg.

Aromatic chilli-spiced okra and coconut stir-fry

Stir-fried okra spiced with mustard, cumin and red chillies and sprinkled with coconut makes a great quick supper. The sweetness of the coconut complements the warm spices perfectly.

SERVES 4

600g/1lb 6oz okra
60ml/4 tbsp sunflower oil
1 onion, finely chopped
15ml/1 tbsp mustard seeds
15ml/1 tbsp cumin seeds
2–3 dried red chillies
10–12 curry leaves
2.5ml/½ tsp turmeric
salt and ground black pepper
90g/3½oz freshly grated coconut,
   to garnish
poppadums, rice or naan, to serve

1 Using a sharp knife, cut the okra diagonally into 1cm/½in lengths, then set aside.

2 Heat the sunflower oil in a wok. When hot add the chopped onion and stir-fry over a medium heat for about 5 minutes until softened.

3 Add the mustard seeds, cumin seeds, red chillies and curry leaves to the onions and stir-fry over a high heat for about 2 minutes.

4 Add the okra and turmeric to the wok and continue to stir-fry over a high heat for 3–4 minutes.

5 Remove the wok from the heat, sprinkle over the coconut and season well with salt and ground black pepper. Serve immediately with poppadums, steamed rice or naan bread.

Nutritional information per portion: Energy 191Kcal/790kJ; Protein 5.1g; Carbohydrate 6.2g, of which sugars 5.1g; Fat 16.5g, of which saturates 5.1g; Cholesterol 0mg; Calcium 249mg; Fibre 7.1g; Sodium 15mg.

Thai yellow vegetable curry

This hot and spicy curry made with coconut milk has a creamy richness that contrasts wonderfully with the heat of chilli and the bite of lightly cooked vegetables. Yellow curry paste is available in supermarkets and is useful if you're in a hurry, but it can include shrimp paste and fish sauce, so it is important to check the ingredients before you purchase it.

SERVES 4

30ml/2 tbsp sunflower oil
200ml/7fl oz/scant 1 cup coconut cream
300ml/½ pint/1¼ cups coconut milk
150ml/¼ pint/⅔ cup vegetable stock
200g/7oz snake (yard-long) beans, cut into
   2cm/¾in lengths
200g/7oz baby corn
4 baby courgettes (zucchini), sliced
1 small aubergine (eggplant), cubed or sliced
10ml/2 tsp palm sugar (jaggery)
fresh coriander (cilantro) leaves, to garnish
noodles or rice, to serve

FOR THE CURRY PASTE

10ml/2 tsp hot chilli powder
10ml/2 tsp ground coriander
10ml/2 tsp ground cumin
5ml/1 tsp turmeric
15ml/1 tbsp chopped fresh galangal
10ml/2 tsp finely grated garlic
30ml/2 tbsp finely chopped
   lemon grass
4 red Asian shallots,
   finely chopped
5ml/1 tsp finely chopped lime rind

1 Make the curry paste. Place all the ingredients in a small food processor and blend with 30–45ml/2–3 tbsp of cold water to make a smooth paste. Add a little more water if the paste seems too dry.

2 Heat a large wok over a medium heat and add the sunflower oil. When hot add 30–45ml/2–3 tbsp of the curry paste and stir-fry for 1–2 minutes.

3 Add the coconut cream and cook gently for 8–10 minutes, or until the mixture starts to separate.

4 Add the coconut milk, stock and vegetables and cook gently for 8–10 minutes, until the vegetables are just tender. Stir in the palm sugar, garnish with coriander leaves and serve with noodles or rice.

Nutritional information per portion: Energy 279Kcal/1161kJ; Protein 9.8g; Carbohydrate 17.4g, of which sugars 13.3g; Fat 19.4g, of which saturates 3.6g; Cholesterol 5mg; Calcium 99mg; Fibre 3.3g; Sodium 824mg.

Avial with roasted coconut

Originally from southern India, this delicious dish is made with firm vegetables, roots and gourds, all cut into bitesize pieces. It is substantial and flexible – choose your own assortment of vegetables, such as pumpkin, butternut squash, winter melon, yams, aubergines (eggplants) or beans.

SERVES 4

2–3 green chillies, seeded and chopped

25g/1oz fresh root ginger, peeled and chopped

5–10ml/1–2 tsp roasted cumin seeds

10ml/2 tsp sugar

5–10ml/1–2 tsp ground turmeric

1 cinnamon stick

5ml/1 tsp salt

2 carrots, cut into bitesize sticks

2 sweet potatoes, cut into bitesize sticks

2 courgettes (zucchini), partially peeled in strips, seeded and cut into bitesize sticks

1 green plantain, peeled and cut into bitesize sticks

a small coil of snake (yard-long) beans or a handful of green beans, cut into bitesize sticks

a handful fresh curry leaves

1 fresh coconut, grated

250ml/8fl oz/1 cup Greek (US strained plain) yogurt

salt and ground black pepper

1 Using a mortar and pestle or food processor, grind the chillies, ginger, cumin seeds and sugar to a paste.

2 In a heavy pan, bring 450ml/15fl oz/scant 2 cups water to the boil. Stir in the turmeric, cinnamon stick and salt. Add the carrots and cook for 1 minute.

3 Add the sweet potatoes and cook for 2 minutes. Add the courgettes, plantain and beans and cook for a further 2 minutes.

4 Reduce the heat, stir in the spice paste and curry leaves, and cook gently for 4–5 minutes, until the vegetables are tender but not mushy, and the liquid has reduced.

5 Stir in half the coconut. Take the pan off the heat and fold in the yogurt. Season to taste. Quickly roast the remaining coconut in a heavy pan over a high heat, until browned. Sprinkle a little over the avial in the pan, and serve the rest with spoonfuls of avial and flatbread.

Nutritional information per portion: Energy 419Kcal/1753kJ; Protein 9.9g; Carbohydrate 47.7g, of which sugars 19.4g; Fat 23g, of which saturates 16.9g; Cholesterol 0mg; Calcium 176mg; Fibre 9g; Sodium 104mg.

Aubergines with lemon grass and coconut milk

Aubergines are pretty to look at and delicate in flavour. They are particularly tasty cooked in coconut milk with lots of chillies, ginger and lemon grass. Serve this with plain jasmine or coconut rice and/or chunks of fresh, crusty bread.

SERVES 4

15ml/1 tbsp ground turmeric
5ml/1 tsp chilli powder
3 slender aubergines (eggplants),
   cut into wedges
45ml/3 tbsp vegetable oil
2 lemon grass stalks, trimmed, halved
   and bruised
600ml/1 pint/2¹/₂ cups coconut milk
salt and ground black pepper
a small bunch fresh coriander (cilantro),
   roughly chopped, to garnish
jasmine or coconut rice, to serve

FOR THE SPICE PASTE

4–6 dried red chillies, soaked in warm water
   until soft, squeezed dry and seeded
4 garlic cloves, chopped
4 shallots, chopped
25g/1oz root ginger, peeled and chopped
2 lemon grass stalks, trimmed and chopped

1 First make the spice paste. Using a mortar and pestle, grind the dried red chillies, garlic, shallots, ginger and lemon grass to a coarse paste.

2 Mix the turmeric and chilli powder together. Rub the mixture all over the aubergine wedges.

3 Heat the oil in a wok or heavy pan. Stir in the spice paste and lemon grass. Add the aubergine wedges, and cook until lightly browned.

4 Pour in the coconut milk, stir well, and bubble it up to thicken. Reduce the heat and cook gently for 15–20 minutes until tender but not mushy. Season with salt and pepper to taste. Sprinkle the coriander over the top and serve straight from the wok. Serve with jasmine or coconut rice.

VARIATION

This works especially well with orange aubergines, if they are available.

Nutritional information per portion: Energy 154Kcal/644kJ; Protein 6.2g; Carbohydrate 11.9g, of which sugars 11g; Fat 9.5g, of which saturates 1.4g; Cholesterol 38mg; Calcium 175mg; Fibre 3g; Sodium 497mg.

Roasted vegetables with a peanut sauce

Served as a vegetable side dish or as a main course, a selection of roasted vegetables in a peanut sauce, enhanced by chillies, soy sauce and other flavourings, is a great favourite throughout South-east Asia. Serve it as a snack with bread, or as a meal with plain boiled rice.

SERVES 4

1 long, slender aubergine (eggplant),
    partially peeled and cut into long strips
2 courgettes (zucchini), partially peeled
    and cut into long strips
1 thick, long sweet potato, cut into strips
2 leeks, trimmed, halved widthways
    and lengthways
2 garlic cloves, chopped
25g/1oz root ginger, peeled and chopped
60ml/4 tbsp vegetable oil
salt
30ml/3 tbsp roasted peanuts, ground,
    to garnish
fresh crusty bread, to serve

FOR THE SAUCE

4 garlic cloves, chopped
2–3 red chillies, seeded and chopped
115g/4oz/1 cup roasted peanuts, crushed
15–30ml/1–2 tbsp dark soy sauce
juice of 1 lime
5–10ml/1–2 tsp Chinese rice vinegar
10ml/2 tsp palm sugar or clear honey
salt and ground black pepper

1 Preheat the oven to 200°C/400°F/ Gas 6. Arrange the vegetables in a shallow oven dish. Using a mortar and pestle, grind the garlic and ginger to a paste, and smear it over the vegetables. Sprinkle with salt and pour over the oil.

2 Place the dish in the oven for 45 minutes, until the vegetables are tender – toss them in the oil halfway through cooking.

3 Meanwhile, make the sauce. Using a mortar and pestle, grind the garlic and chillies to a paste and beat in the peanuts.

4 Stir in the soy sauce, lime juice, vinegar and sugar or honey, and blend with a little water so that the sauce is the consistency of cream.

5 Season with salt and pepper and adjust the sweet and sour balance to taste. Arrange the roasted vegetables on a plate. Drizzle the sauce over them, or serve it separately in a bowl.

6 Sprinkle the ground peanuts over the top of the vegetables and serve warm, or at room temperature, with fresh crusty bread to mop up the garlicky peanut sauce.

Nutritional information per portion: Energy 361Kcal/1502kJ; Protein 11.9g; Carbohydrate 22.7g, of which sugars 11.1g; Fat 25.4g, of which saturates 4.1g; Cholesterol 0mg; Calcium 76mg; Fibre 6.9g; Sodium 292mg.

Silver threads of longevity

The 'silver threads' of the recipe title are cellophane noodles. These are also known as glass noodles, transparent vermicelli or translucent noodles. Here they are teamed with lily buds, which contribute a mild, sweet taste and a deliciously crunchy texture.

SERVES 4

50g/2oz dried lily buds
150g/5oz cellophane noodles
45ml/3 tbsp vegetable oil
30ml/2 tbsp crushed garlic
100g/3¾oz/½ cup beansprouts
30ml/2 tbsp vegetarian oyster sauce
30ml/2 tbsp light soy sauce
45ml/3 tbsp sesame oil
200ml/7fl oz/scant 1 cup water
chopped fresh coriander (cilantro),
    to garnish

1 Soak the lily buds in a bowl of warm water for 30 minutes or until soft. Meanwhile, soak the cellophane noodles in a separate bowl of warm water for 15 minutes.

2 Drain the lily buds, rinse them under cold water and drain again. Snip off the hard ends. Drain the noodles. Using a pair of scissors or a sharp knife, chop the strands into shorter lengths for easier handling.

3 Heat the oil in a wok and fry the garlic for 40 seconds, taking care not to burn it. Add the beansprouts. Stir-fry vigorously for 1 minute. Add the lily buds and the noodles and toss over the heat for 2 minutes.

4 Add the oyster sauce, soy sauce, sesame oil and the water. Toss over the heat until the liquid is hot and coats the noodles. Garnish with coriander and serve immediately.

Nutritional information per portion: Energy 307kcal/1274kJ; Protein 3.3g; Carbohydrate 34.8g, of which sugars 3.4g; Fat 16.7g, of which saturates 2.2g; Cholesterol 0mg; Calcium 15mg; Fibre 0.6g; Sodium 663mg.

Buddhist vegetarian noodles

During Buddhist festivals in China, this dish takes centre stage as temple chefs cook huge cauldrons of it to serve to devotees, free of charge. It is a simple and comforting dish that is redolent with flavour and has a lovely crunchy texture.

SERVES 4

10 dried Chinese black mushrooms

4 pieces sweet dried beancurd wafers

300g/11oz rice vermicelli

45ml/3 tbsp vegetable oil

30ml/2 tbsp crushed garlic

1 large onion, thinly sliced

115g/4oz drained canned bamboo shoots,
    sliced into thin strips

100g/3³⁄₄oz/¹⁄₂ cup beansprouts

115g/4oz Chinese long beans or
    green beans, sliced into thin strips

30ml/2 tbsp hoi sin sauce

30ml/2 tbsp oyster sauce

30ml/2 tbsp dark soy sauce

45ml/3 tbsp sesame oil

400ml/14fl oz/1²⁄₃ cups water

1 Soak the dried mushrooms in a bowl of boiling water for 20–30 minutes until soft. Meanwhile soak the beancurd wafers and rice vermicelli until soft, following the directions on the packets.

2 Drain the mushrooms thoroughly, then cut off and discard the stems and slice the caps into thin strips. Drain the beancurd wafers and slice them thinly. Drain the noodles and set them aside.

3 Heat the oil in a wok and fry the garlic for 40 seconds, until light brown. Add the onion and stir-fry for 2 minutes, then add the bamboo shoots, beansprouts, beans and mushrooms. Stir-fry for 1 minute, then stir in the hoi sin sauce, oyster sauce, soy sauce and sesame oil.

4 Add the beancurd wafers to the wok and stir-fry for 2 minutes more. Add the noodles and pour in the water. Toss over the heat for about 4 minutes, until all the ingredients are cooked and the mixture is well blended. Spoon into a bowl and serve.

COOK'S TIP
The mushroom soaking water can be substituted for some of the water added at the end of cooking. Strain it first, to remove any pieces of grit.

Nutritional information per portion: Energy 509kcal/2116kJ; Protein 12.7g; Carbohydrate 73g, of which sugars 9.9g; Fat 18.6g, of which saturates 2.2g; Cholesterol 0mg; Calcium 200mg; Fibre 3.3g; Sodium 726mg.

Side Dishes

This chapter features dishes that will make

perfect accompaniments to the meals

presented in the preceding chapter, as well

as to those that are already in your

repertoire. From warming traditional

classics, like Potatoes and Parsnips with

Garlic and Cream, through to fragrant and

exotic recipes, such as Aubergine Pilaff with

Cinnamon and Mint, you will be sure to find

the ideal side dish for every meal.

Potato, onion and garlic gratin

This is a simple but delicious way of cooking potatoes and onions together, and is especially good when served with a vegetarian quiche and a simple side salad.

SERVES 4–6

40g/1½oz/3 tbsp butter or 45ml/3 tbsp
   olive oil
2–4 garlic cloves, finely chopped
900g/2lb waxy potatoes, thinly sliced
450g/1lb onions, thinly sliced
450ml/¾ pint/scant 2 cups
   vegetable stock
salt and ground black pepper

1 Use half the butter or oil to grease a 1.5 litre/2½ pint/6¼ cup gratin dish. Preheat the oven to 180°C/350°F/Gas 4.

2 Sprinkle a little of the chopped garlic over the base of the dish and then layer the potatoes and onions in the dish, seasoning each layer with a little salt and pepper and adding the remaining garlic. Finish with a layer of overlapping potato slices on top.

3 Bring the stock to the boil in a pan and pour it over the gratin. Dot the top with the remaining butter, or drizzle the remaining olive oil over the top. Cover tightly with foil and bake for 1½ hours.

4 Increase the oven temperature to 200°C/400°F/Gas 6. Uncover the gratin and then cook for a further 35–50 minutes, until the potatoes are completely cooked and the top layer is browned and crusty. Serve straight from the oven.

Nutritional information per portion: Energy 181Kcal/762kJ; Protein 3.5g; Carbohydrate 30.1g, of which sugars 6.2g; Fat 6.1g, of which saturates 3.8g; Cholesterol 15mg; Calcium 29mg; Fibre 2.6g; Sodium 69mg.

Potatoes baked with fennel and saffron

Potatoes, fennel and onions infused with garlic, saffron and spices make a sophisticated and attractive accompaniment for an egg-based main-course dish.

SERVES 4–6

500g/1¼lb small waxy potatoes, cut
   into chunks or wedges
good pinch of saffron threads
   (12–15 threads)
1 head of garlic, separated into cloves
12 small red or yellow onions, peeled but
   left whole
3 fennel bulbs, cut into wedges, feathery
   tops reserved
4–6 fresh bay leaves
6–9 fresh thyme sprigs
175ml/6fl oz/¾ cup vegetable stock
30ml/2 tbsp sherry vinegar
2.5ml/½ tsp sugar
5ml/1 tsp fennel seeds, lightly crushed
2.5ml/½ tsp paprika
45ml/3 tbsp olive oil
salt and ground black pepper

1 Boil the potatoes in salted water for 8–10 minutes. Drain. Preheat the oven to 190°C/375°F/Gas 5. Soak the saffron in 30ml/2 tbsp warm water for 10 minutes.

2 Peel and finely chop 2 garlic cloves. Place the potatoes, onions, unpeeled garlic cloves, fennel wedges, bay leaves and thyme sprigs in a roasting dish.

3 Mix together the stock, saffron and its soaking liquid, vinegar and sugar, then pour over the vegetables. Stir in the fennel seeds, paprika, garlic and oil, and season with salt and pepper.

4 Cook in the oven for 1–1¼ hours, stirring occasionally, until the vegetables are tender. Chop the reserved fennel, sprinkle over the vegetables and serve.

Nutritional information per portion: Energy 162Kcal/676kJ; Protein 4.4g; Carbohydrate 23.6g, of which sugars 7.1g; Fat 6.2g, of which saturates 0.9g; Cholesterol 0mg; Calcium 49mg; Fibre 4.9g; Sodium 23mg.

Potatoes and parsnips with garlic and cream

For the best results when cooking this dish, cut the potatoes and parsnips very thinly – use a mandolin if you have one. The garlic in this gratin adds a real kick and the combination of cheese and cream makes this a comforting and decadent accompaniment to any meal.

SERVES 4–6

3 large potatoes, total weight about
    675g/1¹/₂lb
350g/12oz small to medium-sized parsnips
200ml/7fl oz/scant 1 cup single (light) cream
100ml/3¹/₂fl oz/scant ¹/₂ cup milk
2 garlic cloves, crushed

butter, for greasing
about 5ml/1 tsp freshly
    grated nutmeg
75g/3oz/³/₄ cup coarsely grated
    Cheddar or Red Leicester cheese
salt and ground black pepper

1 Peel the potatoes and parsnips and cut them into thin slices. Cook in a large pan of salted boiling water for 5 minutes. Drain and cool slightly.

2 Meanwhile, pour the cream and milk into a heavy pan and add the crushed garlic. Bring to the boil over a medium heat, then remove from the heat and leave to stand for about 10 minutes.

3 Preheat the oven to 180°C/350°F/Gas 4 and lightly butter the bottom and sides of a shallow ovenproof dish.

4 Arrange the potatoes and parsnips in the dish, sprinkling each layer with a little freshly grated nutmeg, salt and ground black pepper.

5 Pour the liquid into the dish and press the potatoes and parsnips down into it. Cover with lightly buttered foil and cook in the hot oven for 45 minutes.

6 Remove the foil and sprinkle the grated cheese over the vegetables in an even layer.

7 Return the dish to the oven and continue cooking, uncovered, for a further 20–30 minutes, or until the potatoes and parsnips are tender and the top is golden brown.

Nutritional information per portion: Energy 241kcal/1012kJ; Protein 7.8g; Carbohydrate 27.2g, of which sugars 6.4g; Fat 11.7g, of which saturates 7.2g; Cholesterol 31mg; Calcium 173mg; Fibre 3.9g; Sodium 126mg.

Cauliflower cheese

The use of flour to thicken sauces began in France in the 17th century – hence the French name "roux" for the mixture of flour and fat that forms the basis of a white sauce – but cheese sauce made in this way is a staple of English cooking, as in this traditional dish.

SERVES 4

1 medium cauliflower
25g/1oz/2 tbsp butter
25g/1oz/4 tbsp plain (all-purpose) flour
300ml/½ pint/1¼ cups milk
115g/4oz mature (sharp) Cheddar or
    Cheshire cheese, grated
salt and ground black pepper

1 Trim the cauliflower and cut it into florets. Bring a pan of lightly salted water to the boil, drop in the cauliflower and cook for between 5–8 minutes or until just tender. Drain and tip the florets into an ovenproof dish.

2 To make the sauce, melt the butter in a pan, stir in the flour and cook gently, stirring constantly, for about 1 minute, making sure that the sauce does not brown.

3 Remove the sauce from the heat and gradually stir in the milk. Return the pan to the heat and cook, stirring, until the mixture thickens and comes to the boil. Simmer gently for 1–2 minutes.

4 Stir in three-quarters of the cheese and season to taste. Spoon the sauce over the cauliflower and scatter the remaining cheese on top. Put under a hot grill (broiler) until golden brown.

Nutritional information per portion: Energy 318kcal/1318kJ; Protein 17.4g; Carbohydrate 4.4g, of which sugars 3.9g; Fat 25.8g, of which saturates 16.3g; Cholesterol 71mg; Calcium 371mg; Fibre 1.8g; Sodium 453mg

Carrot and parsnip purée

The most widely used root vegetable, carrots mix well with all the others. They are tasty roasted in chunks, either alone or as a side dish with swede (rutabaga) and parsnip. Carrot and parsnips work especially well together and are often found in a soup, or in this popular side dish.

SERVES 6–8

350g/12oz carrots
450g/1lb parsnips
pinch of freshly grated nutmeg
15g/¹⁄₂oz/1 tbsp butter
about 15ml/1 tbsp single (light)
    cream (optional)
1 small bunch parsley leaves, chopped
    (optional), plus extra to garnish
salt and ground black pepper

1 Peel the carrots and slice fairly thinly. Peel the parsnips and cut them into bitesize chunks (they are softer and will cook more quickly than the carrots). Boil the two vegetables, separately, in salted water, until tender.

2 Drain them well and put them through a mouli-légumes (food mill) with the nutmeg, a good seasoning of salt and black pepper and the butter.

3 Purée the parsnips and carrots together and taste for seasoning.

4 If you like, blend in some cream to taste, and add some freshly chopped parsley for extra flavour.

5 Transfer the carrot and parsnip purée to a warmed serving bowl, generously sprinkle over the freshly chopped parsley to garnish, and serve immediately.

Nutritional information per portion: Energy 92Kcal/385kJ; Protein 1.8g; Carbohydrate 14.1g, of which sugars 8.7g; Fat 3.5g, of which saturates 1.8g; Cholesterol 7mg; Calcium 48mg; Fibre 4.9g; Sodium 38mg

Colcannon

This traditional Irish dish is especially associated with Hallowe'en, when it is likely to be made with curly kale and would have a ring hidden in it – predicting marriage during the coming year.

SERVES 6–8

450g/1lb potatoes, peeled and boiled
450g/1lb curly kale or cabbage, cooked
milk, if necessary
50g/2oz/2 tbsp butter, plus extra
    for serving
1 large onion, finely chopped
salt and ground black pepper

1 Mash the potatoes. Chop the kale or cabbage, add it to the potatoes and mix. Stir in a little milk if the mash is too stiff.

2 Melt a little butter in a frying pan over a medium heat and add the onion. Cook until softened. Remove and mix well with the potato and kale or cabbage.

3 Add the remainder of the butter to the hot pan. When very hot, turn the potato mixture on to the pan and spread it out. Fry until brown, then cut it roughly into pieces and continue frying until they are crisp and brown.

4 Serve in bowls or as a side dish, with plenty of butter.

Nutritional information per portion: Energy 306Kcal/1281kJ; Protein 5.4g; Carbohydrate 40.6g, of which sugars 13.6g; Fat 14.6g, of which saturates 8.8g; Cholesterol 36mg; Calcium 104mg; Fibre 5.9g; Sodium 127mg

Vegetable Ragoût

The vegetables in this dish are cooked until soft and the result is a deliciously buttery combination of flavours. Serve as a side dish or a light lunch with dark rye bread on the side.

SERVES 4

3–4 carrots
1 swede (rutabaga)
1 turnip
1 parsnip
10ml/2 tsp sunflower oil
1 large onion, finely chopped
100–200ml/3½–7fl oz/scant ½–1 cup
    vegetable stock or lightly salted water
105ml/7 tbsp finely chopped
    fresh parsley
15g/½oz/1 tbsp butter
dark rye bread and butter, to serve

1 Cut the carrots, swede, turnip and parsnip into small chunks. Heat the oil in a flameproof casserole, add the chopped onion and fry over a medium heat, for 3–5 minutes until softened.

2 Add the carrots, swede, turnip and parsnip to the pan and fry, stirring frequently, for a further 10 minutes.

3 Add the stock and bring to the boil. Cover with a lid and simmer for 20 minutes until the vegetables are soft.

4 Add the chopped parsley and the butter to the pan and stir until the butter has melted and is coating the vegetables. Season with salt to taste and serve hot, with rye bread.

Nutritional information per portion: Energy 122kcal/506kJ; Protein 2.6g; Carbohydrate 15.9g, of which sugars 13.3g; Fat 5.7g, of which saturates 2.3g; Cholesterol 8mg; Calcium 137mg; Fibre 6.3g; Sodium 68mg.

Braised leeks with carrots

Sweet carrots and leeks go well together and are good finished with a little chopped mint, chervil or parsley. This is a good accompaniment to a hearty vegetable pie.

SERVES 6

65g/2¹/₂oz/5 tbsp butter
675g/1¹/₂lb carrots, thickly sliced
2 fresh bay leaves
pinch of caster (superfine) sugar
75ml/5 tbsp water
675g/1¹/₂lb leeks, cut into 5cm/2in
    lengths
120ml/4fl oz/¹/₂ cup white wine
30ml/2 tbsp chopped fresh mint, chervil
    or parsley
salt and ground black pepper

1 Melt 25g/1oz/2 tbsp of the butter in a pan and cook the carrots gently, without allowing them to brown, for 4–5 minutes.

2 Add the bay leaves, seasoning, the sugar and water. Bring to the boil, cover and cook for 10–15 minutes, until the carrots are tender. Uncover, then boil until the juices have evaporated.

3 Meanwhile, melt another 25g/1oz/2 tbsp of the butter in a pan that will take the leeks in a single layer. Add the leeks and fry them in the butter over a low heat for 4–5 minutes, without browning.

4 Add seasoning, a good pinch of sugar, the wine and half the chopped herbs. Heat until simmering, then cover and cook gently for 5–8 minutes, until the leeks are tender, but not collapsed.

5 Uncover the leeks and turn them in the buttery juices. Increase the heat, then boil the liquid rapidly until reduced to a few tablespoons.

6 Add the carrots to the leeks and reheat them gently, then swirl in the remaining butter. Season, if necessary. Transfer to a warmed serving dish and serve sprinkled with the remaining chopped herbs.

Nutritional information per portion: Energy 163Kcal/677kJ; Protein 3.8g; Carbohydrate 18.5g, of which sugars 16.4g; Fat 6.5g, of which saturates 3.6g; Cholesterol 13mg; Calcium 87mg; Fibre 7.8g; Sodium 85mg.

Braised lettuce and peas with spring onions and mint

This is based on the traditional French way of braising peas with lettuce and spring onions in butter. It is a delicious accompaniment to a simple main course.

SERVES 4

50g/2oz/¼ cup butter

4 Little Gem (Bibb) lettuces,
    halved lengthways

2 bunches spring onions (scallions),
    trimmed

5ml/1 tsp caster (superfine) sugar

400g/14oz shelled peas (about
    1kg/2¼lb in pods)

4 fresh mint sprigs

120ml/4fl oz/½ cup vegetable stock
    or water

15ml/1 tbsp chopped fresh mint,
    to garnish

salt and ground black pepper

1 Melt half the butter in a heavy pan over a low heat. Add the lettuces and spring onions.

2 Turn the vegetables in the butter, then sprinkle in the sugar, 2.5ml/½ tsp salt and plenty of black pepper.

3 Cover the pan, and cook very gently for 5 minutes, stirring once. Add the peas and mint sprigs, stirring them into the buttery juices.

4 Pour in the vegetable stock or water, then cover and cook over a gentle heat for a further 5 minutes. Uncover the pan and increase the heat to reduce the liquid to a few tablespoons.

5 Stir in the remaining butter and adjust the seasoning to taste. Transfer to a warmed serving dish and sprinkle with the chopped mint. Serve immediately.

Nutritional information per portion: Energy 161Kcal/670kJ; Protein 9.1g; Carbohydrate 15.9g, of which sugars 6.8g; Fat 7.4g, of which saturates 3.7g; Cholesterol 13mg; Calcium 73mg; Fibre 6.5g; Sodium 47mg.

Stir-fried kai lan

There was a time when this popular Chinese vegetable was practically unobtainable outside its country of origin, but airfreight has changed all that and most Chinese food stores now stock it. Known as Chinese broccoli – kai lan in Cantonese – it actually bears little resemblance to broccoli, being more closely related to kale. It has dark green leaves and crunchy stems.

SERVES 4

350g/12oz kai lan (Chinese broccoli)
30ml/2 tbsp vegetable oil
30ml/2 tbsp shredded fresh root ginger
30ml/2 tbsp crushed garlic
30ml/2 tbsp vegetarian oyster sauce
30ml/2 tbsp Chinese wine

1 Separate the kai lan leaves from the stalks. Cut each leaf in half. Trim the stalks, then peel them thinly, removing any tough portions of outer skin. Slice each stalk diagonally in half.

2 Bring a pan of water to the boil and blanch the kai lan leaves for 1 minute. Drain immediately in a colander, and refresh under cold water. This will help to retain the vegetable's bright green colour.

3 Repeat the boiling and draining process with the kai lan stalks, making sure to keep the leaves and stalks separate.

4 Heat the oil in a wok and fry the ginger and garlic until the latter is golden brown. Add the kai lan stalks and stir-fry for 1 minute. Add the leaves, stir well, then add the oyster sauce and wine. Stir rapidly over the heat for 2 minutes, spoon into a dish and serve immediately.

Nutritional information per portion: Energy 108kcal/448kJ; Protein 5g; Carbohydrate 5.9g, of which sugars 3.7g; Fat 6.4g, of which saturates 0.8g; Cholesterol 0mg; Calcium 53mg; Fibre 2.9g; Sodium 131mg.

Braised Chinese leaves

Chinese leaves, also known as Chinese cabbage, taste delicious in a salad or stir-fry and need little seasoning apart from soy sauce as they have a natural sweet flavour. This dish is somewhat soupy, since the leaves contribute extra liquid. It is often served with rice porridge, and keeps well. A delicious and authentic addition to a vegetarian Chinese banquet that is simple to prepare.

SERVES 4–6

1 head Chinese leaves (Chinese cabbage)
30ml/2 tbsp sesame oil
300ml/½ pint/1¼ cups water
5ml/1 tsp ground black pepper
30ml/2 tbsp light soy sauce

1 Slice the Chinese leaves lengthways and remove the hard tip and core. Cut the leaves into 2.5cm/1in slices and place in a colander. Rinse under cold running water, then drain thoroughly.

2 Mix the oil, water, black pepper and soy sauce in a wok. Bring to simmering point, add the Chinese leaves and braise for 15 minutes over a medium heat. Spoon into a heated dish and serve immediately.

Nutritional information per portion: Energy 58kcal/239kJ; Protein 1.3g; Carbohydrate 4.6g, of which sugars 4.5g; Fat 3.8g, of which saturates 0.5g; Cholesterol 0mg; Calcium 42mg; Fibre 1.8g; Sodium 362mg.

Peas cooked in olive oil

Peas cooked in this way can be included in a delicious frittata, or mixed with a little warmed cream to dress pasta, with just a sprinkling of freshly grated Parmesan cheese and black pepper to finish it off. The peas are soaked first, which means that they soften without cooking, and their natural sweetness develops perfectly. A truly adaptable dish.

SERVES 4

1.2kg/2¹/₂lb fresh peas in their pods, or 450g/1lb shelled peas
100ml/3¹/₂fl oz/scant ¹/₂ cup olive oil
1 onion, thinly sliced
2.5ml/¹/₂ tsp caster (superfine) sugar
sea salt and ground black pepper

1 Soak the peas in cold water for 1 hour.

2 Meanwhile, put the olive oil in a flameproof casserole or heavy pan and add the sliced onion. Fry the onion over a low heat for about 10 minutes, or until it has softened and turned golden brown in colour.

3 Drain the peas and add to the onion. Add the sugar, season with salt and pepper, then cover and cook gently until soft and cooked through. The timing will depend on how large or small the peas are: tiny ones will take about 4 minutes; larger, fat peas with tougher skins could take up to 15 minutes.

Nutritional information per portion: Energy 280kcal/1157kJ; Protein 9g; Carbohydrate 21.3g, of which sugars 8.9g; Fat 18.4g, of which saturates 2.7g; Cholesterol 0mg; Calcium 49mg; Fibre 6.7g; Sodium 4mg.

Green beans with tomatoes and dill

This delicious dish can be served at room temperature as part of a meze spread, hot as a side dish to accompany grilled or barbecued vegetables, or as a main course with a dollop of creamy yogurt. It is best served with yogurt and lots of warm, fresh crusty bread to mop up the sauce. The taste of fresh dill is an essential part of the dish.

SERVES 4

1–2 onions, roughly chopped

2 garlic cloves, roughly chopped

30–45ml/2–3 tbsp olive oil

500g/1¼lb stringless runner (green) beans, trimmed and each cut into 3–4 pieces

15ml/1 tbsp sugar

juice of 1 lemon

2 x 400g/14oz cans chopped tomatoes

a handful of fresh dill, roughly chopped

salt and ground pepper

1 Put the onions, garlic and oil in a wide heavy pan and stir over a low heat until they soften. Toss in the beans, coating them in the onions and oil, then stir in the sugar and lemon juice.

2 Add the tomatoes and bring to the boil, then lower the heat and add the dill. Cook gently for 35–40 minutes, or until the beans are tender and the tomato sauce is fairly thick.

3 Season with salt and pepper to taste before serving.

Nutritional information per portion: Energy 141kcal/588kJ; Protein 4.5g; Carbohydrate 16.5g, of which sugars 14g; Fat 6.8g, of which saturates 1.1g; Cholesterol 0mg; Calcium 75mg; Fibre 5.7g; Sodium 20mg.

Potatoes baked with tomatoes, olives and feta

This dish is baked in an earthenware dish and is a fabulous accompaniment to a barbecue. Or serve it on its own as a main course with a squeeze of lemon, a dollop of yogurt and a green salad.

SERVES 4–6

675g/1½lb organic new potatoes
15ml/1 tbsp butter
45ml/3 tbsp olive oil
2 red onions, cut into quarters, and sliced
    along the grain
3–4 garlic cloves, chopped
5–10ml/1–2 tsp cumin seeds, crushed
5–10ml/1–2 tsp Turkish red (bell) pepper
10ml/2 tsp dried oregano
10ml/2 tsp sugar
15ml/1 tbsp white wine vinegar
400g/14oz can chopped tomatoes,
    drained of juice
12–16 black olives
115g/4oz feta cheese, crumbled
salt and ground black pepper
extra olive oil, for drizzling
1 lemon, cut into wedges, and natural
    (plain) yogurt, to serve (optional)

1 Preheat the oven to 200°C/400°F/ Gas 6. Put the potatoes into a pan of cold water, bring to the boil and cook for 15–20 minutes, until tender. Drain and refresh under cold running water, then peel and cut the potatoes into thick slices or bitesize wedges.

2 Heat the butter and 30ml/2 tbsp of the oil in a heavy pan, stir in the onions and garlic and cook until soft.

3 Add the cumin, red pepper and oregano to the pan then stir in the sugar and vinegar, followed by the tomatoes. Season to taste.

4 Put the potatoes and olives into a baking dish – preferably an earthenware one – and spoon the tangy tomato mixture over the top of them.

5 Crumble the feta over the top and sprinkle with a little more oregano. Drizzle over the remaining oil, then bake in the oven for 25–30 minutes.

6 Serve the dish straight from the oven, with lemon wedges to squeeze over and a dollop of yogurt, if you like.

Nutritional information per portion: Energy 243kcal/1016kJ; Protein 6.3g; Carbohydrate 27.5g, of which sugars 9.3g; Fat 12.8g, of which saturates 5g; Cholesterol 19mg; Calcium 102mg; Fibre 2.9g; Sodium 447mg.

Sweet potatoes in coconut and ginger paste

Sweet potatoes and beetroot take on a wonderful sweetness when roasted, and they are delicious with the savoury onions and aromatic coconut, ginger and garlic paste.

SERVES 4

30ml/2 tbsp groundnut oil
450g/1lb sweet potatoes, peeled and cut
    into thick strips or chunks
4 beetroot (beets), cooked, peeled and
    cut into wedges
450g/1lb small red onions, halved
5ml/1 tsp coriander seeds, lightly crushed
3–4 small whole fresh red chillies
salt and ground black pepper
chopped coriander (cilantro), to garnish

FOR THE PASTE

2 large garlic cloves, chopped
1–2 green chillies, seeded and chopped
15ml/1 tbsp chopped fresh root ginger
45ml/3 tbsp chopped coriander (cilantro)
75ml/5 tbsp coconut milk
30ml/2 tbsp groundnut oil
grated rind of ½ lime
2.5ml/½ tsp light muscovado (brown)
    sugar

1 First make the paste. Process the garlic, chillies, ginger, coriander and coconut milk in a food processor, blender or coffee grinder.

2 Turn the paste into a small bowl and beat in the oil, lime rind and muscovado sugar. Preheat the oven to 200°C/400°F/Gas 6.

3 Heat the oil in a roasting pan in the oven for 5 minutes. Add the sweet potatoes, beetroot, onions and coriander seeds, tossing them in the hot oil. Roast for 10 minutes.

4 Stir in the paste and the whole red chillies. Season well with salt and pepper, and toss the vegetables to coat them thoroughly with the garlic and chilli paste.

5 Roast the vegetables for a further 25–35 minutes, or until the sweet potatoes and onions are fully cooked and tender. Stir 2–3 times to prevent the paste from sticking to the pan.

6 Serve immediately, sprinkled with a little chopped fresh coriander.

Nutritional information per portion: Energy 272Kcal/1143kJ; Protein 4.4g; Carbohydrate 39.8g, of which sugars 19.2g; Fat 11.8g, of which saturates 1.7g; Cholesterol 0mg; Calcium 98mg; Fibre 6.3g; Sodium 122mg.

Red onions with cheese and tomato butter

Onions roast to a wonderful sweet creaminess when cooked in their skins. They need butter, lots of black pepper and a savoury main course to set off their sweetness.

SERVES 6

6 even-sized red onions, unpeeled

175–225g/6–8oz crumbly cheese (such as Lancashire, Caerphilly or Cheshire), thinly sliced

a few chopped chives

salt and ground black pepper

FOR THE SUN-DRIED TOMATO BUTTER

115g/4oz butter, softened

65g/2½oz sun-dried tomatoes in olive oil, drained and finely chopped

30ml/2 tbsp chopped fresh basil or parsley

1 Preheat the oven to 180°C/350°F/Gas 4. Put the unpeeled onions in a roasting pan and roast for 1¼–1½ hours, until they are tender and feel soft when lightly squeezed.

2 Meanwhile, prepare the sun-dried tomato butter. Cream the butter and then beat in the tomatoes and basil or parsley. Season to taste with salt and pepper and shape into a roll, then wrap in foil and chill.

3 Slit the tops of the onions and open them up. Season with plenty of black pepper and add chunks of the sun-dried tomato butter. Sprinkle the cheese and chives over the top and eat immediately, mashing the butter and cheese into the soft, sweet onion.

Nutritional information per portion: Energy 345kcal/1427kJ; Protein 10.7g; Carbohydrate 17.5g, of which sugars 12.8g; Fat 25.7g, of which saturates 16.7g; Cholesterol 72mg; Calcium 290mg; Fibre 3.5g; Sodium 389mg.

Stewed tomatoes and red peppers

This pepper stew is really delicious, either as a side dish or as part of an antipasto. It can even be added to beaten eggs and turned into a flavoursome frittata, and is also good with cheese.

SERVES 4

450g/1lb ripe tomatoes

45ml/3 tbsp extra virgin olive oil

1 onion, sliced

450g/1lb red (bell) peppers, seeded and sliced

sea salt

1 First, peel the tomatoes. Place the tomatoes in a large heatproof bowl and cover with boiling water. Leave for 30 seconds, then carefully drain them. The skins should peel off easily. Chop the flesh, discarding the seeds.

2 Put the oil in a pan and fry the onion for 5 minutes, or until softened but not browned.

3 Add the sliced peppers, stir, and cook for 10 minutes.

4 Add the chopped tomatoes, season with salt and stir well. Simmer the mixture gently, stirring frequently, for about 30 minutes, or until the peppers and tomatoes have softened completely.

Nutritional information per portion: Energy 129kcal/538kJ; Protein 1.9g; Carbohydrate 10.7g, of which sugars 10.4g; Fat 9g, of which saturates 1.4g; Cholesterol 0mg; Calcium 17mg; Fibre 2.9g; Sodium 15mg.

Stewed beans

Delicious hot or cold, this recipe can be served on its own or as part of another dish – on top of toasted bread as crostini, or alongside vegetable or egg dishes. It is a very adaptable bean dish that can be made with canned or dried beans, or fresh beans when they are in season.

SERVES 4

45–60ml/3–4 tbsp olive oil

3 cloves garlic, peeled and crushed

2 or 3 leaves fresh sage

400g/14oz can cannellini beans, drained

200g/7oz canned tomatoes, strained

sea salt and ground black pepper

1 Put the oil in a pan and gently fry the garlic and sage.

2 When the oil is golden brown, add the drained cannellini beans and season with a generous pinch of ground black pepper.

3 Stir the mixture together thoroughly, then add the strained tomatoes. Simmer gently for a further 20 minutes.

4 Check and adjust the seasoning to taste, then serve.

Nutritional information per portion: Energy 160kcal/669kJ; Protein 6.3g; Carbohydrate 14.6g, of which sugars 2.7g; Fat 8.9g, of which saturates 1.3g; Cholesterol 0mg; Calcium 19mg; Fibre 5.1g; Sodium 425mg.

Refried beans

These beans are not actually fried twice, but they are cooked twice, first by boiling them until tender and then by frying in butter. These are much better than canned refried beans, which can be rather bland, and they make the perfect accompaniment to a traditional Mexican meal.

SERVES 4

250g/9oz/1¼ cups dried pinto beans, soaked overnight in water to cover

1.75 litres/3 pints/7½ cups water

25g/1oz/2 tbsp butter

2 onions, finely chopped

5ml/1 tsp ground cumin

5ml/1 tsp ground coriander

3 garlic cloves, crushed

small bunch of fresh coriander (cilantro) or 4–5 dried avocado leaves

50g/2oz feta cheese

salt

1 Drain the beans, rinse and drain again. Put the water in a pan, bring to the boil and add the beans. Lower the heat and simmer for 1½ hours, until the beans are tender and there is only a little liquid remaining.

2 Melt the butter in a frying pan. Add the onions, cumin and ground coriander. Cook gently for 30 minutes or until the onions caramelize.

3 Add a ladleful of the cooked beans. Fry them for a few minutes to heat.

4 Mash the beans into the onions as they cook using a fork. Gradually add the beans, then stir in the garlic.

5 Lower the heat and cook the beans to form a thick paste. Season with salt and transfer to a serving dish.

6 Strip the leaves from the fresh coriander and chop them, or crumble the avocado leaves, and sprinkle most of them over the beans. Crumble the feta cheese over, then garnish with the reserved leaves.

Nutritional information per portion: Energy 279kcal/1174kJ; Protein 16.9g; Carbohydrate 32.8g, of which sugars 5.4g; Fat 9.9g, of which saturates 4.4g; Cholesterol 15mg; Calcium 148mg; Fibre 11.3g; Sodium 197mg.

Garlic-flavoured lentils with carrots and sage

Serve these garlicky lentils with grilled or barbecued vegetable kebabs, or on their own with a dollop of yogurt seasoned with crushed garlic, salt and pepper, and lemon wedges.

SERVES 4–6

175g/6oz/¾ cup green lentils, rinsed and
　picked over
45–60ml/3–4 tbsp fruity olive oil
1 onion, cut in half lengthways, in half again
　crossways, and sliced along the grain
3–4 plump garlic cloves, roughly chopped
　and bruised with the flat side of a knife
5ml/1 tsp coriander seeds
a handful of dried sage leaves
5–10ml/1–2 tsp sugar
4 carrots, sliced
15–30ml/1–2 tbsp tomato purée (paste)
salt and ground black pepper
1 bunch of fresh sage or flat leaf parsley,
　to garnish

1 Bring a pan of water to the boil and tip in the lentils. Lower the heat, partially cover the pan and simmer for 10 minutes. Drain and rinse well under cold running water.

2 Heat the oil in a heavy pan, stir in the onion, garlic, coriander, sage and sugar, and cook until the onion begins to colour. Toss in the carrots and cook for 2–3 minutes.

3 Add the lentils and pour in 250ml/8fl oz/1 cup water, making sure the lentils and carrots are covered. Stir in the tomato purée and cover the pan, then cook the lentils and carrots gently for about 20 minutes, until most of the liquid has been absorbed. The lentils and carrots should both be tender, but still have some bite. Season with salt and pepper to taste.

4 Garnish the lentils with the fresh sage or flat leaf parsley, and serve hot or at room temperature.

Nutritional information per portion: Energy 166kcal/696kJ; Protein 7.6g; Carbohydrate 21.1g, of which sugars 6.7g; Fat 6.2g, of which saturates 0.9g; Cholesterol 0mg; Calcium 38mg; Fibre 4g; Sodium 22mg.

Aubergine pilaff with cinnamon and mint

This wonderful rice and aubergine dish is made with olive oil and served cold. Eat it on its own, accompanied by a green salad, or serve it with grilled or barbecued vegetables.

SERVES 4–6

2 large aubergines (eggplants)
30–45ml/2–3 tbsp olive oil
30–45ml/2–3 tbsp pine nuts
1 large onion, finely chopped
5ml/1 tsp coriander seeds
30ml/2 tbsp currants, soaked in warm
　　water for 5–10 minutes and drained
10–15ml/2–3 tsp sugar
15–30ml/1–2 tbsp ground cinnamon
15–30ml/1–2 tbsp dried mint
1 small bunch of fresh dill, finely chopped
3 tomatoes, skinned, seeded and chopped
350g/12oz/generous 1³/₄ cups long or
　　short grain rice, well rinsed and drained
sunflower oil, for deep-frying
juice of ¹/₂ lemon
salt and ground black pepper
fresh mint sprigs and lemon wedges,
　　to serve

1 Use a vegetable peeler to peel the aubergines lengthways, in stripes like a zebra. Quarter them lengthways, then slice each quarter into bitesize chunks and place in a bowl of salted water. Cover, and leave to soak for 30 minutes.

2 Heat the olive oil in a pan, stir in the pine nuts and cook until golden. Add the onion and soften it, then stir in the coriander seeds and currants. Add the sugar, cinnamon, mint and dill and stir in the tomatoes.

3 Add the rice, then pour in 900ml/1¹/₂ pints/3³/₄ cups water, season and bring to the boil. Lower the heat, then simmer for 10–12 minutes, until most of the water has been absorbed. Turn off the heat, cover the pan with a cloth and press the lid tightly on top. Leave the rice to steam for about 15 minutes.

4 Heat enough sunflower oil for deep-frying in a wok. Drain and squeeze the aubergines, then toss them in batches in the oil, for a few minutes at a time. When they are golden, lift them out with a slotted spoon and drain.

5 Transfer the rice to a serving bowl and toss the aubergine chunks through it with the lemon juice. Garnish with fresh mint sprigs and serve warm or cold, with lemon wedges for squeezing.

Nutritional information per portion: Energy 369kcal/1539kJ; Protein 6.1g; Carbohydrate 52.2g, of which sugars 11g; Fat 15.2g, of which saturates 1.8g; Cholesterol 0mg; Calcium 38mg; Fibre 2.7g; Sodium 8mg.

Desserts and Bakes

Unlike other courses, dessert has almost no restrictions for the vegetarian. This chapter features some delicious and decadent ways to finish a meal, as well as tempting sweet bakes and savoury breads. Included are light and refreshing options, such as Summer Berry Tart, and Tropical Scented Red and Orange Fruit Salad, as well as some comforting and truly indulgent dishes, like Sticky Pear Pudding, and Deep Dish Apple Pie.

Cheesecake with sour cherries

This cheesecake is from Belgium, and the base is traditionally made using Belgium's favourite cookie – speculaas – while the creamy topping is studded with cherries and spiked with Kriek beer.

SERVES 6–8

500g/1¼lb jar stoned (pitted) Morello
   cherries in syrup
60m/4 tbsp water
30ml/2 tbsp powdered gelatine
150ml/¼ pint/⅔ cup Kriek beer, such as St.
   Louis, Belle-Vue or Lindemans
500g/1¼lb/2¼ cups Quark, soft cheese or
   fromage frais
150ml/¼ pint/⅔ cup crème fraîche or
   sour cream
200ml/7fl oz/scant 1 cup double
   (heavy) cream

115g/4oz/generous ½ cup caster
   (superfine) sugar
90ml/6 tbsp flaked (sliced) almonds, to
   decorate (optional)

FOR THE CRUST

200g/7oz speculaas cookies (spice cookies)
   or other biscuits (cookies) suitable
   for crumbing
100g/3½oz/scant ½ cup
   unsalted butter
30ml/2 tbsp cherry jam (optional)

1 Make the crust. Crumb the cookies in a food processor or put them between sheets of baking parchment and crush with a rolling pin. Transfer to a bowl.

2 Melt the butter in a pan and stir it into the crumbs with the jam, if using. Mix well. Using clean hands, shape into a ball. Place in a 23cm/9in springform cake tin (pan) and press out to form an even base. Cover with clear film (plastic wrap) and place in the refrigerator.

3 Drain the cherries in a colander, reserving the syrup in a measuring jug (cup). Chop 115g/4oz/⅔ cup of the cherries and set them aside. Leave the remaining cherries in the colander.

4 Put the water in a cup and sprinkle the gelatine on the surface. Put aside until the gelatine is spongy.

5 Pour 150ml/¼ pint/⅔ cup of the syrup from the cherries into a pan. Bring to the boil, then cool for 30 seconds. Whisk in the gelatine until dissolved. Stir in the Kriek beer and strain the mixture into a jug (pitcher).

6 In a large bowl, beat the Quark, soft cheese or fromage frais with the crème fraîche or sour cream, and gradually add the gelatine mixture. Fold in the reserved chopped cherries.

7 Whip the cream with the sugar in a bowl, until stiff peaks form. Carefully fold it into the cheese and cream mixture.

8 Spoon the filling over the crumb base in the pan and smooth the top with a wetted spoon or spatula. Cover with clear film. Chill in the refrigerator for at least 4 hours or overnight.

9 Remove the cheesecake from the tin and transfer it to a serving platter. Sprinkle the flaked almonds over the surface of the cheesecake and press some on to the sides. Serve in slices, with the remaining drained cherries.

Nutritional information per portion: Energy 574kcal/2394kJ; Protein 6.5g; Carbohydrate 50.1g, of which sugars 39g; Fat 39.5g, of which saturates 24.9g; Cholesterol 87mg; Calcium 145mg; Fibre 0.7g; Sodium 198mg.

Tropical scented red and orange fruit salad

This fresh fruit salad is perfect after a rich, heavy meal. It is a great dish to serve in early summer, as it is the end of the orange season and the beginning of the strawberry season.

SERVES 4–6

350–400g/12–14oz/3–3½ cups
   strawberries, hulled and halved
3 oranges, peeled and segmented
3 small blood oranges, peeled
   and segmented
1–2 passion fruit
120ml/4fl oz/½ cup dry white wine
sugar, to taste

1 Put the strawberries and oranges into a serving bowl. Halve the passion fruit and spoon the flesh into the fruit.

2 Pour the wine over the fruit and add sugar to taste. Toss gently and then chill until ready to serve.

COOK'S TIP
Use a sharp knife to segment the oranges. First remove the top and bottom of the orange, then work around the orange in downwards slices, removing the skin and pith from the orange's circumference. Finally, cut between the membranes to remove each segment individually.

Nutritional information per portion: Energy 81Kcal/342kJ; Protein 2g; Carbohydrate 15.6g, of which sugars 15.6g; Fat 0.2g, of which saturates 0g; Cholesterol 0mg; Calcium 75mg; Fibre 3g; Sodium 13mg.

Boston banoffee pie

This sumptuous combination of deliciously biscuity pastry, fudge-toffee filling and sliced banana topping will prove irresistible, and is wonderfully easy to make.

SERVES 6

115g/4oz/¹/₂ cup butter, diced

200g/7oz can skimmed, sweetened
  condensed milk

115g/4oz/¹/₂ cup soft brown sugar

30ml/2 tbsp golden (light corn) syrup

2 small bananas, sliced

a little lemon juice

whipped cream, to decorate

5ml/1 tsp grated plain
  (semisweet) chocolate

FOR THE PASTRY

150g/5oz/1¹/₄ cups plain
  (all-purpose) flour

115g/4oz/¹/₂ cup butter, diced

50g/2oz/¹/₄ cup caster (superfine) sugar

1 Preheat the oven to 160°C/325°F/ Gas 3. In a food processor, process the flour and diced butter until crumbed. Stir in the caster sugar and mix to form a soft, pliable dough.

2 Press into a 20cm/8in loose-based flan tin (pan). Bake for 30 minutes.

3 To make the filling, place the butter in a pan with the condensed milk, brown sugar and syrup. Heat gently, stirring, until the butter has melted and the sugar has dissolved.

4 Bring to a gentle boil and cook for 7–10 minutes, stirring constantly, until the mixture thickens and turns a light caramel colour.

5 Pour the hot caramel filling into the pastry case and leave until completely cold. Sprinkle the banana slices with lemon juice and arrange in overlapping circles on top of the filling, leaving a gap in the centre. Pipe a generous swirl of whipped cream in the centre and sprinkle with the grated chocolate.

Nutritional information per portion: Energy 608Kcal/2547kJ; Protein 6.4g; Carbohydrate 78.5g, of which sugars 58.9g; Fat 32g, of which saturates 20.1g; Cholesterol 82mg; Calcium 246mg; Fibre 0.8g; Sodium 211mg.

Summer berry tart

A simple crisp pastry case is all that is needed to set off this classic filling of vanilla-flavoured custard topped with luscious berry fruits. A true taste of summer.

SERVES 6–8

3 egg yolks
50g/2oz/¼ cup caster (superfine) sugar
30ml/2 tbsp cornflour (cornstarch)
30ml/2 tbsp plain (all-purpose) flour
5ml/1 tsp vanilla essence (extract)
300ml/½ pint/1¼ cups milk
150ml/¼ pint/⅔ cup double (heavy) cream
800g/13/4lb/4½–5 cups mixed summer
    berries, such as raspberries, blueberries,
    loganberries or boysenberries
60ml/4 tbsp redcurrant jelly

30ml/2 tbsp raspberry liqueur
fresh mint leaves, to
    decorate (optional)

FOR THE PASTRY
185g/6½oz/1⅔ cups plain (all-purpose)
    flour, plus extra for dusting
pinch of salt
115g/4oz/½ cup butter, diced
1 egg yolk
30ml/2 tbsp chilled water

1 To make the pastry, sift the flour and salt into a mixing bowl. Rub or cut in the butter until the mixture resembles fine breadcrumbs. Mix the egg yolk with the chilled water and sprinkle over the dry ingredients. Mix to a firm dough.

2 Put the dough on to a lightly floured surface and knead for a few seconds, until smooth. Wrap in clear film (plastic wrap) and chill for 30 minutes.

3 Roll out the pastry and use to line a 25cm/10in petal-shaped flan tin (quiche pan) or a 23cm/9in round pan. Wrap in clear film and chill.

4 Put a baking sheet in the oven and preheat to 200°C/400°F/Gas 6. Prick the base of the pastry, line with foil and baking beans and bake for 15 minutes. Remove the foil and beans and bake for 10 minutes more. Leave to cool.

5 Beat the egg yolks, sugar, cornflour, flour and vanilla together. Bring the milk to the boil in a pan. Slowly pour on to the egg mixture, whisking all the time.

6 Pour the custard into the cleaned pan and cook over a low heat, stirring constantly, until it has thickened. Return to a clean mixing bowl, cover the surface with a piece of clear film and set aside to cool. Whip the cream until thick, then fold into the custard. Spoon the custard into the pastry case and spread out evenly.

7 Arrange the fruit on top of the custard. Gently heat the redcurrant jelly and liqueur together until melted. Allow to cool, then brush over the fruit. Serve the tart within 3 hours of assembling, decorated with mint, if using.

COOK'S TIP
If you are planning to serve the tart within an hour or so of filling, you can finish the fruit with a simple dusting of icing sugar instead of the glaze.

Nutritional information per portion: Energy 394Kcal/1644kJ; Protein 6.5g; Carbohydrate 36.4g, of which sugars 12.5g; Fat 25.7g, of which saturates 15g; Cholesterol 159mg; Calcium 125mg; Fibre 1.9g; Sodium 121mg.

Baked bananas with ice cream

Baked bananas make the perfect partners for delicious vanilla ice cream topped with a toasted hazelnut sauce. This is quick and easy for times when only sweet treats will do.

SERVES 4

4 large bananas
15ml|/1 tbsp lemon juice
4 large scoops of vanilla ice cream

FOR THE SAUCE
25g/1oz/2 tbsp unsalted butter
50g/2oz/¹⁄₂ cup hazelnuts, toasted and roughly chopped
45ml/3 tbsp golden (light corn) syrup
30ml/2 tbsp lemon juice

1 Preheat the oven to 180°C/350°F/Gas 4. Place the unpeeled bananas on a baking sheet and brush them with the lemon juice.

2 Bake for about 20 minutes until the skins are turning black and the flesh gives a little when the bananas are gently squeezed.

3 Meanwhile, make the sauce. Melt the butter in a pan. Add the hazelnuts and cook for 1 minute. Add the syrup and lemon juice and heat, stirring, for 1 minute more.

4 To serve, slit each banana open and transfer to serving plates. Serve with ice cream and the sauce poured over.

Nutritional information per portion: Energy 382Kcal/1598kJ; Protein 5.4g; Carbohydrate 49.4g, of which sugars 45.7g; Fat 18.6g, of which saturates 7.6g; Cholesterol 28mg; Calcium 88mg; Fibre 2.1g; Sodium 106mg.

Apple-stuffed crêpes

Sweet apples make the perfect filling for these crêpes that are made from cider-infused batter. But they can also be made with a variety of other sweet fillings, such as succulent strawberries.

SERVES 4

115g/4oz/1 cup plain (all-purpose) flour
pinch of salt
2 large (US extra large) eggs
175ml/6fl oz/³⁄₄ cup milk
120ml/4fl oz/¹⁄₂ cup sweet cider
butter, for frying
4 eating apples
60ml/4 tbsp caster (superfine) sugar
120ml/8 tbsp clear honey, and 150ml/¹⁄₄
    pint/²⁄₃ cup double (heavy) cream,
    to serve

1 Sift the flour and salt into a bowl. Beat in the eggs and milk. Add the cider. Stand for 30 minutes.

2 Melt a little butter in a small frying pan. Ladle in enough batter to coat the pan thinly. Cook for 1 minute until it is golden, then flip it over and cook the other side until golden. Repeat until you have used up the batter. Set the crêpes aside and keep warm.

3 Core the apples and cut them into thick slices. Heat 15g/¹⁄₂oz butter in a frying pan. Add the apples to the pan and cook until golden. Transfer to a bowl and sprinkle with sugar.

4 Fold each pancake in half, then fold in half again to form a cone. Fill each with some of the fried apples. Place two filled pancakes on each dessert plate. Drizzle with a little honey and serve with cream.

Nutritional information per portion: Energy 489Kcal/2057kJ; Protein 8.2g; Carbohydrate 71.5g, of which sugars 49.6g; Fat 20.1g, of which saturates 11.3g; Cholesterol 139mg; Calcium 137mg; Fibre 2.1g; Sodium 69mg.

Sticky pear pudding

Ground cloves add a distinctive fragrant flavour to this decadent hazelnut, pear and coffee pudding which is served with a delicate citrus-scented orange cream.

SERVES 6

30ml/2 tbsp ground coffee

15ml/1 tbsp near-boiling water

50g/2oz/¹/₂ cup toasted skinned hazelnuts

4 ripe pears

juice of ¹/₂ orange

115g/4oz/8 tbsp butter, softened

115g/4oz/generous ¹/₂ cup golden caster (superfine) sugar, plus an extra 15ml/1 tbsp, for baking

2 eggs, beaten

50g/2oz/¹/₂ cup self-raising (self-rising) flour

pinch of ground cloves

8 whole cloves, optional

45ml/3 tbsp maple syrup

fine strips of orange rind, to decorate

FOR THE ORANGE CREAM

300ml/¹/₂ pint/1¹/₄ cups whipping cream

15ml/1 tbsp icing (confectioners') sugar, sifted

finely grated rind of ¹/₂ orange

1 Preheat the oven to 180°C/350°F/Gas 4. Lightly grease a 20cm/8in shallow cake tin (pan). Put the ground coffee in a small bowl and pour the water over. Leave to infuse for 4 minutes, then strain through a fine sieve (strainer).

2 Grind the hazelnuts in a coffee grinder until fine. Peel, halve and core the pears. Thinly slice the pear halves part of the way through. Brush with orange juice.

3 Beat the butter and the 115g/4oz/generous ¹/₂ cup caster sugar together in a bowl until light and fluffy. Gradually beat in the eggs, then fold in the flour, ground cloves, hazelnuts and coffee. Spoon into the tin and level the surface.

4 Pat the pears dry on kitchen paper, then arrange in the sponge mixture, flat side down. Lightly press 2 whole cloves into each pear half. Brush the pears with 15ml/1 tbsp maple syrup. Sprinkle the pears with the 15ml/1 tbsp caster sugar. Bake for 45–50 minutes or until firm and well-risen.

5 While the sponge is cooking, make the orange cream. Whip the cream, icing sugar and orange rind until soft peaks form. Spoon into a serving dish and chill until needed.

6 Allow the sponge to cool for 10 minutes in the tin, then remove and place on a serving plate. Brush with the remaining maple syrup and decorate with orange rind. Serve warm with the cream.

Nutritional information per portion: Energy 852Kcal/3571kJ; Protein 12.5g; Carbohydrate 107g, of which sugars 45g; Fat 44.5g, of which saturates 23.8g; Cholesterol 169mg; Calcium 362mg; Fibre 5.3g; Sodium 493mg.

Deep dish apple pie

The addition of a deliciously buttery caramel to the apples in this classic dish takes it one step further and, coupled with the mixed spice, gives a rich flavour to the juices in the pie.

SERVES 6

900g/2lb eating apples
75g/3oz/6 tbsp unsalted butter
45–60ml/3–4 tbsp demerara (raw) sugar
3 cloves
2.5ml/½ tsp mixed (apple pie) spice

FOR THE PASTRY
250g/9oz/2¼ cups plain (all-purpose)
   flour, plus extra for dusting
pinch of salt
125g/5oz/10 tbsp unsalted butter,
   chilled and diced
30–45ml/2–3 tbsp chilled water
a little milk, for brushing
caster (superfine) sugar, for dredging
clotted cream, ice cream or double
   (heavy) cream, to serve

1 Preheat the oven to 200°C/400°F/Gas 6. Sift together the flour and salt. Rub in the butter until the mixture resembles breadcrumbs. Stir in enough chilled water to bring the pastry together. Knead lightly then wrap in clear film (plastic wrap) and chill for 30 minutes.

2 Peel, core and thickly slice the apples. Melt the butter in a frying pan, add the sugar and cook for 3–4 minutes to caramelize. Add the apples and stir to coat. Cook until the apples take on a little colour, add the spices and tip out into a bowl.

3 Divide the pastry in two and, on a lightly floured surface, roll out into two rounds. Line a 23cm/9in pie plate with one round of pastry. Spoon in the filling and mound up in the centre. Cover with the remaining pastry, sealing and crimping the edges. Make a 5cm/2in long slit through the top of the pastry. Brush with milk and dredge with caster sugar.

4 Place the pie on a baking sheet and bake in the oven for between 25–35 minutes until golden and firm. Serve with clotted cream, ice cream or double cream.

Nutritional information per portion: Energy 591Kcal/2488kJ; Protein 7.4g; Carbohydrate 89.9g, of which sugars 39.8g; Fat 25g, of which saturates 15.3g; Cholesterol 62mg; Calcium 117mg; Fibre 4.4g; Sodium 193mg.

Blueberry frangipane flan

There's something irresistible about this tangy lemon pastry case with its sweet almond filling and rings of ripe blueberries. The jam and liqueur glaze adds an indulgent finish.

SERVES 6

30ml/2 tbsp ground coffee
45ml/3 tbsp near-boiling milk
50g/2oz/¼ cup butter
50g/2oz/¼ cup caster (superfine) sugar
1 egg
115g/4oz/1 cup ground almonds
15ml/1 tbsp plain (all-purpose) flour
225g/8oz/2 cups blueberries
30ml/2 tbsp seedless blackberry jam
15ml/1 tbsp Amaretto liqueur
crème fraîche or sour cream, to serve

FOR THE PASTRY

175g/6oz/1½ cups plain (all-purpose)
   flour, plus extra for dusting
115g/4oz/½ cup butter, diced
25g/1oz/2 tbsp caster (superfine) sugar
finely grated rind of ½ lemon
15ml/1 tbsp chilled water

1 Preheat the oven to 190°F/375°C/Gas 5. Sift the flour into a bowl and rub in the butter. Add the sugar and lemon rind, stir, then add the water and mix to a firm dough. Wrap the pastry in clear film (plastic wrap) and chill for 20 minutes.

2 Roll out the pastry on a floured surface and line a 23cm/9in loose-based flan tin (pan). Prick with a fork. Line the pastry with baking parchment and baking beans and bake for 10 minutes. Remove the parchment and beans and bake for 10 minutes more. Remove from the oven.

3 Mix the coffee and milk in a bowl. Leave to infuse for 4 minutes. Cream the butter and sugar until pale. Beat in the egg, then add the almonds and flour. Strain in the coffee through a sieve (strainer) and gently fold it in.

4 Spoon the mixture into the case. Gently press the blueberries into the filling. Bake for 30 minutes, cover with foil after 20 minutes.

5 Remove from the oven and cool slightly. Melt the jam and liqueur and brush over the flan. Remove from the tin and serve warm.

Nutritional information per portion: Energy 523Kcal/2180kJ; Protein 8.9g; Carbohydrate 44.9g, of which sugars 20.2g; Fat 34.8g, of which saturates 15.6g; Cholesterol 91mg; Calcium 132mg; Fibre 3.6g; Sodium 162mg.

Chocolate potato cake

The secret ingredient mashed potato makes this rich cake especially moist and delicious. Use a good-quality dark chocolate for best results and serve with whipped cream.

MAKES A 23CM/9IN CAKE

oil, for greasing
200g/7oz/1 cup sugar
250g/9oz/1 cup and 2 tbsp butter
4 eggs, separated
275g/10oz dark (bittersweet) chocolate
75g/3oz/3/4 cup ground almonds
165g/51/2 oz mashed potato

225g/8oz/2 cups self-raising
 (self-rising) flour
5ml/1 tsp cinnamon
45ml/3 tbsp milk
white and dark (bittersweet) chocolate
 shavings, to garnish
whipped cream, to serve

1 Preheat the oven to 180°C/350°F/Gas 4. Grease and line a 23cm/9in round cake tin (pan) with baking parchment.

2 Cream the sugar and 225g/8oz/1 cup of the butter until pale. Beat in egg yolks one at a time until smooth and creamy.

3 Grate 175g/6oz of the chocolate and stir it into the mixture with the ground almonds. Pass the mashed potato through a sieve (strainer) and stir it into the mixture. Sift together the flour and cinnamon and fold into the mixture with the milk.

4 Whisk the egg whites until they hold stiff but not dry peaks, and fold into the cake mixture.

5 Spoon into the prepared tin and smooth over, but make a slight hollow in the middle to help keep the surface of the cake level. Bake in the oven for 11/4 hours until a wooden toothpick inserted in the centre comes out clean. Allow the cake to cool in the tin, then turn out and cool on a wire rack.

6 Melt the remaining chocolate in a heatproof bowl over a pan of hot water. Add the remaining butter in cubes and stir well until the chocolate has melted and the mixture is smooth and glossy.

7 Peel off the lining paper and trim the top of the cake so that it is level. Smooth over the icing and allow to set. Decorate with white and dark chocolate shavings and serve with whipped cream.

Nutritional information per cake: Energy 5749Kcal/24034kJ; Protein 87.1g; Carbohydrate 590.9g, of which sugars 391.8g; Fat 354.8g, of which saturates 188.1g; Cholesterol 1465mg; Calcium 1408mg; Fibre 21.5g; Sodium 2731mg.

Frosted carrot and parsnip cake

The grated carrots and parsnips in this deliciously light and crumbly cake help to keep it moist and account for its very good keeping qualities. The creamy sweetness of the cooked meringue topping makes a wonderful contrast to the cake's light crumb.

SERVES 8–10

oil, for greasing

1 lemon

1 orange

15ml/1 tbsp caster (superfine) sugar

225g/8oz/1 cup butter

225g/8oz/1 cup soft light brown sugar

4 eggs

225g/8oz/1²⁄₃ cups carrot and parsnip, grated

115g/4oz/1¼ cups sultanas (golden raisins)

225g/8oz/2 cups self-raising (self-rising) wholemeal (whole-wheat) flour

5ml/1 tsp baking powder

FOR THE TOPPING

50g/2oz/¼ cup caster (superfine) sugar

1 egg white

1 Preheat the oven to 180°C/350°F/Gas 4. Lightly grease a 20cm/8in loose-based cake tin (pan) and line the base with a circle of baking parchment.

2 Finely grate the lemon and orange. Put about half of the rind, selecting the longest shreds, in a bowl and mix with the caster sugar. Arrange the sugar-coated rind on a sheet of baking parchment and leave in a warm place, to dry.

3 Cream the butter and sugar until pale and fluffy. Add the eggs gradually, then beat well. Stir in the unsugared rinds, the grated carrots and parsnips, 30ml/2 tbsp orange juice and the sultanas.

4 Gradually fold in the flour and baking powder, and tip into the prepared tin. Bake for 1½ hours until risen, golden and just firm. Leave the cake to cool in the tin, then turn out on to a serving plate.

5 To make the topping, place the caster sugar in a bowl over boiling water with 30ml/2 tbsp of the orange juice. Stir until the sugar begins to dissolve. Remove from the heat, add the egg white and salt, and whisk for 1 minute with an electric beater. Return to the heat and whisk for 6 minutes until the mixture becomes stiff and glossy, holding a good shape. Allow to cool slightly, whisking frequently.

6 Swirl the cooked meringue topping over the cake and leave to firm up for about 1 hour. To serve, sprinkle with the sugared lemon and orange rind, which should be dry and crumbly.

Nutritional information per portion: Energy 540Kcal/2265kJ; Protein 7.5g; Carbohydrate 71.5g, of which sugars 50.5g; Fat 26.9g, of which saturates 15.7g; Cholesterol 174mg; Calcium 156mg; Fibre 1.8g; Sodium 333mg.

Pecan cake

This cake is traditionally served with sweetened boiled milk – but whipped cream or crème fraîche can be used instead. Serve the cake with a few redcurrants for a splash of uplifting colour.

SERVES 8–10

115g/4oz/1 cup pecan nuts
115g/4oz/1/2 cup butter, softened
115g/4oz/1/2 cup soft light brown sugar
5ml/1 tsp natural vanilla extract
4 large (US extra large) eggs, separated
75g/3oz/3/4 cup plain (all-purpose) flour
pinch of salt
12 whole pecan nuts, to decorate
whipped cream or crème fraîche

FOR DRIZZLING

50g/2oz/1/4 cup butter
120ml/4fl oz/scant 1/2 cup clear honey

1 Preheat the oven to 180°C/350°F/Gas 4. Grease a 20cm/8in round cake tin (pan). Toast the nuts in a pan for 5 minutes, shaking frequently. Grind finely.

2 Cream the butter with the sugar in a mixing bowl, then beat in the vanilla extract and egg yolks.

3 Add the flour to the ground nuts and mix well. Whisk the egg whites with the salt in a grease-free bowl until soft peaks form. Fold the whites into the butter mixture, then fold in the flour and nut mixture. Spoon the mixture into the cake tin and bake for 30 minutes. Cool the cake in the tin for 5 minutes, then remove the sides of the tin. Stand the cake on a wire rack until cold.

4 Remove the cake from the base of the tin if necessary, then return it to the rack and arrange the pecans on top. Transfer to a plate. Melt the butter in a small pan, add the honey and bring to the boil, stirring. Lower the heat and simmer for 3 minutes. Pour over the cake. Serve with whipped cream or crème fraîche.

Nutritional information per portion: Energy 428Kcal/1785kJ; Protein 6.2g; Carbohydrate 34.7g, of which sugars 27.4g; Fat 30.5g, of which saturates 12.5g; Cholesterol 158mg; Calcium 51mg; Fibre 1g; Sodium 170mg.

Courgette and double-ginger cake

Both fresh and preserved ginger are used to flavour this unusual teabread. It is delicious served warm, cut into thick slices and spread with butter or margarine.

SERVES 8–10

3 eggs

225g/8oz/generous 1 cup caster
    (superfine) sugar

250ml/8fl oz/1 cup sunflower oil

5ml/1 tsp vanilla extract

15ml/1 tbsp syrup from a jar of
    stem ginger

225g/8oz courgettes (zucchini), grated

2.5cm/1in piece fresh root ginger, grated

350g/12oz/3 cups unbleached plain
    (all-purpose) flour

5ml/1 tsp baking powder

pinch of salt

5ml/1 tsp ground cinnamon

2 pieces stem ginger, chopped

15ml/1 tbsp demerara (raw) sugar

1 Preheat the oven to 190°C/325°F/Gas 5. Beat together the eggs and sugar until light and fluffy. Slowly beat in the oil until the mixture forms a batter. Mix in the vanilla extract and ginger syrup, then stir in the courgettes and fresh ginger.

2 Sift together the flour, baking powder and salt into a large bowl. Add the cinnamon and mix well, then stir the remaining dried ingredients into the courgette mixture.

3 Lightly grease a 900g/2lb loaf tin (pan) and pour in the courgette mixture. Smooth and level the top, then sprinkle the chopped ginger and demerara sugar over the surface.

4 Bake for 1 hour until a skewer inserted into the centre comes out clean. Leave the cake in the tin to cool for about 20 minutes, then turn out on to a wire rack.

Nutritional information per portion: Energy 502kcal/2107kJ; Protein 7.1g; Carbohydrate 67.3g, of which sugars 34g; Fat 24.6g, of which saturates 3.3g; Cholesterol 71mg; Calcium 95mg; Fibre 1.6g; Sodium 35mg.

Marmalade teabread

A traditional English teabread that's perfect for serving with a cup of tea. The marmalade gives it a lovely flavour, at the same time keeping it moist and allowing it to keep well.

MAKES 8–10 SLICES

200g/7oz/1³/₄ cups plain
   (all-purpose) flour
5ml/1 tsp baking powder
6.25ml/1¹/₄ tsp ground cinnamon
100g/3¹/₂oz/7 tbsp butter, cut into
   small pieces
55g/2oz/3 tbsp soft light brown sugar
1 egg
60ml/4 tbsp chunky orange marmalade
about 45ml/3 tbsp milk
60ml/4 tbsp glacé icing, to decorate
shreds of orange and lemon rind,
   to decorate

1 Preheat the oven to 160°C/325°F/Gas 3. Grease a 450g/1lb loaf tin (pan), and line with baking parchment.

2 Sift the flour, baking powder and cinnamon together, then rub in the butter and stir in the sugar.

3 Beat the egg lightly in a small bowl and mix it with the marmalade and the milk.

4 Mix the milk mixture into the flour, to give a soft consistency.

5 Transfer the mixture into the prepared tin, put into the hot oven and cook for about 1¹/₄ hours, until the cake is firm and springy to the touch and cooked through.

6 Leave the cake to cool for 5 minutes, then turn on to a wire rack. Carefully peel off the lining paper and leave the cake aside to cool completely.

7 Drizzle the glacé icing over the top of the cake and decorate with shreds of orange and lemon rind.

Nutritional information per portion: Energy 250Kcal/1050kJ; Protein 3.5g; Carbohydrate 38g, of which sugars 19g; Fat 10.4g, of which saturates 6.2g; Cholesterol 48mg; Calcium 56mg; Fibre 0.8g; Sodium 86mg.

Fruit loaf

Dried fruit and flaked almonds are delicious in this energy-giving sweet bread. Serve it thickly sliced and spread with good butter to help prepare for the day. A great loaf for weekend breakfasts.

SERVES 8–10

sunflower oil, for greasing

7 egg whites

175g/6oz/scant 1 cup caster (superfine) sugar

115g/4oz/1 cup flaked (sliced) almonds, toasted

115g/4oz/3/4 cup sultanas (golden raisins)

grated rind of 1 lemon

165g/51/2oz/11/3 cups plain (all-purpose) flour, sifted, plus extra for flouring

75g/3oz/6 tbsp butter, melted

1 Preheat the oven to 180°C/350°F/Gas 4 and grease and flour a 1kg/21/4lb loaf tin (pan). Whisk the egg whites until they are very stiff, but not crumbly. Fold in the sugar gradually, then add the almonds, sultanas and lemon rind.

2 Fold the flour and butter into the mixture and tip it into the prepared tin. Bake for about 45 minutes until well risen and pale golden brown. Cool for a few minutes in the tin, then turn out and serve warm or cold, in slices.

Nutritional information per portion: Energy 364Kcal/1529kJ; Protein 8.1g; Carbohydrate 49.9g, of which sugars 33.8g; Fat 16.1g, of which saturates 5.6g; Cholesterol 20mg; Calcium 87mg; Fibre 2g; Sodium 117mg.

Red onion with rosemary focaccia

This bread is rich in olive oil and it has an aromatic topping of red onion, fresh rosemary and coarse salt. Serve it with a tomato and basil salad for the true taste of Italy.

SERVES 4–5

450g/1lb/4 cups strong white bread
    flour, plus extra for dusting
5ml/1 tsp salt
7g/¼oz fresh yeast
2.5ml/½ tsp light muscovado
    (brown) sugar
250ml/8fl oz/1 cup lukewarm water
60ml/4 tbsp extra virgin olive oil, plus
    extra for greasing
5ml/1 tsp very finely chopped fresh
    rosemary, plus 6–8 small sprigs
1 red onion, thinly sliced
coarse salt

1 Sift the flour and salt into a bowl. Set aside. Cream the yeast with the sugar, stir in half the water and set aside in a warm place for 10 minutes.

2 Add the yeast, the remaining water, 15ml/1 tbsp of the oil and the chopped rosemary to the flour. Form a dough, then gather into a ball and knead on a floured surface for 5 minutes, until smooth. Place the dough in a lightly oiled bowl and cover with oiled clear film (plastic wrap) and leave to rise overnight in the refrigerator.

3 Oil a baking sheet. Knead the dough to form a flat loaf that is about 30cm/12in round or square. Place on the baking sheet, cover with oiled film and leave to rise in a warm place for a further 40–60 minutes.

4 Preheat the oven to 220°C/425°F/Gas 7. Toss the onion in 15ml/1 tbsp of the oil and sprinkle over the loaf with the rosemary sprigs and a sprinkling of coarse salt. Bake for 15–20 minutes until golden brown. Serve the bread freshly baked or leave to cool slightly and serve warm.

Nutritional information per portion: Energy 496Kcal/2094kJ; Protein 11g; Carbohydrate 90.4g, of which sugars 3.8g; Fat 12.5g, of which saturates 1.8g; Cholesterol 0mg; Calcium 167mg; Fibre 4g; Sodium 496mg.

Greek olive bread

The flavours of the Mediterranean emanate from this decorative bread, speckled with olives, red onions and herbs. With a bottle of red wine it brings sunshine to the table.

MAKES 2 LOAVES

675g/1½ lb/6 cups unbleached white bread flour, plus extra for dusting
10ml/2 tsp salt
25g/1oz fresh yeast
350ml/12fl oz/1½ cups lukewarm water
75ml/5 tbsp olive oil
175g/6oz/1½ cups pitted black olives, roughly chopped
1 red onion, finely chopped
30ml/2 tbsp chopped fresh coriander (cilantro) or mint

1 Grease two baking sheets. Sift the flour and salt into a bowl and make a well in the centre. Blend the yeast with half of the water. Add to the centre of the flour with the remaining water and the olive oil; mix to a soft dough.

2 Knead the dough on a floured surface for 8–10 minutes. Place in an oiled bowl, cover with oiled clear film (plastic wrap) and leave to rise, in a warm place, for 1 hour. Turn on to a floured surface and knock back (punch down).

3 Roll out the dough. Sprinkle the olives, onion and herbs over the surface, then gently knead together. Cut the dough in half and shape each piece into an oval loaf, about 20cm/8in long. Place on the baking sheets.

4 Brush the centre of each loaf with water and cover with lightly oiled clear film and leave to rise, in a warm place, for about 45 minutes.

5 Preheat the oven to 220°C/425°F/Gas 7. Dust the loaves with flour and bake for 35–40 minutes, until golden. Transfer to a wire rack to cool.

Nutritional information per loaf: Energy 1515Kcal/6392kJ; Protein 33.4g; Carbohydrate 268.2g, of which sugars 9.3g; Fat 41.7g, of which saturates 6.1g; Cholesterol 0mg; Calcium 545mg; Fibre 14.1g; Sodium 3946mg.

The Vegetarian Kitchen

The vegetarian diet makes the most of fresh, seasonal ingredients, and is a true celebration of nature's bounty. This section looks in detail at some of the wonderful ingredients available to the vegetarian cook, including perfectly ripe fruits and vegetables, delicate and fragrant herbs and spices, wholesome and filling beans, pulses and legumes, and highly nutritious dairy and soya products.

Being vegetarian

Many people think that vegetarianism is a relatively new trend, but in many countries around the globe, vegetarianism, in one form or another, has been the natural way to eat for many hundreds, if not thousands, of years. Today, there are millions of people who are vegetarians.

ABOVE: *A balanced vegetarian diet should contain all of the vitamins and minerals that your body needs.*

Defining vegetarianism

There are various forms of vegetarianism: you might be a vegan, a lacto-vegetarian, a fruitarian or on a macrobiotic diet. According to the Vegetarian Society, the definition of a vegetarian is "someone living on a diet of grains, pulses, nuts, seeds, vegetables and fruits with or without the use of dairy products and eggs (preferably free-range)".

BELOW: *For maximum flavour always buy fruit and vegetables when they are in season.*

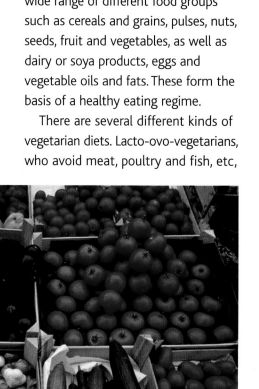

A vegetarian does not eat any meat, poultry, game, fish, shellfish or crustacea, or meat by-products such as gelatine or animal fats.

A typical vegetarian diet includes a wide range of different food groups such as cereals and grains, pulses, nuts, seeds, fruit and vegetables, as well as dairy or soya products, eggs and vegetable oils and fats. These form the basis of a healthy eating regime.

There are several different kinds of vegetarian diets. Lacto-ovo-vegetarians, who avoid meat, poultry and fish, etc, but include dairy products and eggs in their diet, are the most common. Lacto-vegetarians are the same as Lacto-ovo-vegetarians, but they do not eat eggs.

Vegans, on the other hand, follow a much stricter eating regime and do not eat meat, poultry and fish, dairy products, eggs, or any other animal product. Fruitarians eat a diet which consists mainly of raw fruit, grains and nuts. Very few processed or cooked foods are eaten. Finally, some people choose a macrobiotic diet, which is a diet followed for spiritual and philosophical reasons. This specific diet progresses through ten levels, becoming increasingly restrictive. Although not all levels are vegetarian, each level gradually eliminates animal products until the highest level eventually reaches a brown rice diet.

As long as you eat a wide variety of foods, life never need be dull if you choose to follow a vegetarian diet. By its very nature, a balanced vegetarian diet tends to be naturally low in saturated and total fat, high in dietary fibre and complex carbohydrates, and high in many protective vitamins and minerals.

Through vegetarian cooking, you can mix and match the vibrant colours, textures and flavours of vegetables, fruits, pulses and grains with many other exciting ingredients, and experiment with a wide variety of interesting and unusual foods to create all kinds of delicious and tempting dishes from many parts of the world.

Buying vegetarian food

Many vegetarian foods available in shops and supermarkets are clearly marked on their packaging as being 'suitable for vegetarians'. Some food products also carry the 'V' (vegetarian)

BELOW: *Some wine and cheese is not suitable for vegetarians.*

ABOVE: *The vegetarian diet offers a wide variety of flavours, textures and colours.*

symbol and others carry vegetarian indicators familiar to particular countries such as the 'two green leaves' symbol. Some vegetarian foods carry a Vegetarian Society symbol, which indicates that they are approved and meet specific criteria that ensures the foods are absolutely suitable for vegetarians. Other food products, such as cheese, may also include additional useful information, for example advice that the cheese is made using 'non-animal rennet'.

Nutrition and the vegetarian diet

In a vegetarian diet, protein, which is made up of amino acids, is needed for the growth and repair of all body cells. Protein is provided by foods such as eggs, milk, yogurt, cheese and soya bean products, such as tofu and tempeh, all of which contain many of the essential amino acids we need. Beans, peas, lentils and grains are also a valuable source of protein.

Carbohydrates, which divide into simple and complex carbohydrates, supply the body with energy. Simple carbohydrates tend to be found in sugars and sweet foods, which should only be eaten in moderation. Complex carbohydrates on the other hand are a vital part of a healthy diet and are provided by rice, pasta, bread, potatoes and other vegetables, as well as many fruits. Many of these complex carbohydrate foods also provide fibre, vitamins and minerals.

Vitamins and minerals have many vital functions, such as keeping the nervous system healthy, helping to maintain healthy eyes, skin and hair, and to protect against disease. A vegetarian diet should supply many of these, although some vegetarians increase their intake of vitamins and minerals with supplements such as vitamin B12, calcium, iron and zinc.

Vegetables

Naturally low in fat and bursting with vitamins and minerals, vegetables are one food group that should ideally make up the bulk of our diet.

Vegetables play an essential role in the vegetarian diet. They are sometimes served as dishes in their own right, and sometimes as accompaniments. Either way, there is a vast range of imaginative recipes from all over the world, incorporating vegetables, from salads to hearty, robust and warming stews.

ROOTS AND TUBERS

Vegetables such as carrots, swedes, parsnips and potatoes are a comforting and nourishing food, and it is not surprising that they should be popular in the winter. Their sweet, dense flesh provides sustained energy, valuable fibre, vitamins and minerals.

Carrots

The best carrots are summer's sweet new crop. Buy organic carrots if you can because pesticide residues have been found in non-organic ones.

RIGHT: *Deliciously sweet parsnips are ideal for warming winter dishes.*

Look for firm, smooth carrots – the smaller they are, the sweeter they are. They are delicious raw, and can be steamed, stir-fried, roasted or puréed.

Beetroot (beet)

This colourful vegetable adds a vibrant hue and flavour to all sorts of dishes. It is often pickled in vinegar, but is much better roasted, as this emphasizes its sweet earthy flavour.

Parsnips

This vegetable has a sweet, creamy flavour and is delicious roasted, puréed or steamed. Scrub before use and only peel if tough. Avoid large roots, which can be woody.

Celeriac

This knobbly root is closely related to celery, which explains its flavour – a cross between aniseed, celery and parsley. It has ivory flesh and is one of the few root vegetables that must be peeled before use. It can be steamed, baked, combined with potatoes and mashed.

Swedes (rutabaga)

The swede has pale orange flesh with a delicate sweet but earthy flavour. Trim off the thick peel, then treat in the same way as other root vegetables.

Turnips

This humble vegetable has crisp, ivory flesh, which is enclosed in white, green and

BELOW: *Beneath its thick, woody exterior swede has a sweet flavour and delicate orange flesh.*

pink-tinged skin. It has a slightly peppery flavour, the intensity of which depends on their size and the time of harvesting. Steam, bake or use in casseroles and soups.

Potatoes

Small potatoes, such as Pink Fir Apple, Charlotte, and new potatoes, such as Jersey Royals, are best steamed. Main crop potatoes, such as Estima and Maris Piper, are more suited to roasting, baking or mashing, and can be used to make chips (French fries).

ABOVE: *Celeriac has a distinctive flavour, and adds a delicious twist to mashed potatoes.*

Jerusalem artichokes

The Jerusalem artichoke is an entirely different vegetable to the globe artichoke. It is a tuber belonging to the sunflower family. Jerusalem artichokes have a lovely distinctive flavour and are good in vegetarian soups. They are also delicious baked, braised, lightly sautéed or puréed.

BRASSICAS AND GREEN LEAFY VEGETABLES

This large group of vegetables ranges from the crinkly-leafed Savoy cabbage to the small, walnut-sized Brussels sprout. Green, leafy vegetables include spinach, spring greens and Swiss chard.

Broccoli

Two types of brocolli are commonly available: purple-sprouting, which has fine, leafy stems and a delicate head, and calabrese, the more substantial variety with a tightly budded top and thick stalk. Choose broccoli that has

BELOW: Squashes come in a variety of shapes and sizes, buy whichever are in season.

bright, compact florets. If you cook broccoli, steam or stir-fry it to preserve the nutrients and keep the cooking time brief to retain the vivid green colour.

Cauliflowers

The Cauliflower has a mild flavour and cream-coloured compact florets that should be encased in large, bright green leaves. It is delicious tossed in a light vinaigrette dressing or combined with tomatoes and spices.

Cabbages

It is best to eat cabbage raw, or cooked until only just tender. There are several different varieties: Savoy cabbage has substantial, crinkly leaves that are perfect for stuffing; firm white and red cabbages can be shredded and used raw in salads; while pak choi (bok choy) is best cooked in stir-fries or with noodles.

Spinach

Iron-rich spinach is high in fibre which can help to lower harmful levels of LDL cholesterol. Young, tender spinach leaves can be eaten raw and need little preparation, but older leaves should be washed well, then picked over and the tough stalks removed.

PUMPKINS AND SQUASHES

These vegetables come in a tremendous range of shapes, colours and sizes. Squashes are broadly divided into summer and winter types: cucumbers, courgettes and

ABOVE: Cauliflower can be boiled, steamed, or eaten raw.

marrows fall into the summer category, while pumpkins and butternut squashes are winter varieties.

Butternut squash

A large, pear-shaped squash with a golden skin and vibrant orange flesh. The skin is inedible and should be removed along with the seeds. Roast, bake, mash or use in soups or casseroles.

Pumpkins

Sweet pumpkin is used in both dessert and savoury dishes, such as pies, soups, casseroles, soufflés and even ice cream. Avoid boiling pumpkin as it can become waterlogged and soggy.

BELOW: Spinach is rich in iron and fibre.

Courgettes (zucchini)

These summer squash have shiny green skin, a sweet delicate flavour and a crisp texture. They can be sliced or grated and eaten raw, or they can be cooked, combining well with other vegetables such as peppers, tomatoes and aubergines (eggplant).

Cucumbers

Their refreshing, mild flavour makes cucumbers perfect to use raw in salads or thinly sliced as a sandwich filling. However, they can also be pickled and cooked in other ways, such as steaming, baking or stir-frying.

SHOOT VEGETABLES

This highly prized collection of vegetables, each with a distinctive flavour and appearance, ranges from the aristocratic asparagus to the flowerbud-like globe artichoke.

BELOW: *Despite its delicate, leafy fronds fennel has a robust and distinctive aniseed flavour.*

Fennel bulb

This bulb with delicate feathery fronds has a distinctive flavour of aniseed and a crisp, refreshing texture. It can be eaten raw, dressed with vinaigrette or served in a mixed salad.

Asparagus

Spears of asparagus grow from spring to early summer, and is only worth eating during this period. Asparagus spears can be boiled, steamed, grilled (broiled) or roasted in a little olive oil.

Celery

Crisp celery is useful for adding flavour to stocks. Low in calories, but rich in vitamin C and potassium, celery is a diuretic and sedative.

Globe artichokes

Globe artichokes have edible, slightly nutty-flavoured heads (flower buds). Look for artichoke heads with tightly packed leaves, as open leaves indicate that the vegetable is too mature.

VEGETABLE FRUITS

By cultivation and use, tomatoes, aubergines and peppers are all vegetables, but botanically they are classified as fruit.

Tomatoes

An essential ingredient for many vegetarian recipes. The smallest varieties of tomato are sweet and tasty. Medium tomatoes are delicious and good for slicing. Plum tomatoes are ideal for tomato-based sauces. Beefsteaks are the best for stuffing or for slicing for salads.

Peeling tomatoes

Add a professional finish to sauces and soups that are not being sieved (strained) by peeling the tomatoes.

1 Use a small, sharp knife to cut out the green stalk end, then make a cross in the skin on the base of each tomato.

2 Place the tomatoes in a bowl and add boiling water to cover. Leave for 30 seconds, then drain. Cool slightly.

3 Gently pull away the loosened skin from the tomato.

Aubergines (eggplant)

The plump purple variety of aubergine is the most common. They can be grilled (broiled), baked, stuffed, stewed or lightly sautéed, either on their own or with other vegetables, and since they absorb flavours well, they can be used with most seasonings.

(Bell) Peppers

Capsicums, or bell peppers as they are also known, come in a range of colours, though they all have the same sweetish flavour and crunchy texture. They can be eaten raw or cooked in a variety of ways – roasted and dressed with a light olive oil or vinaigrette dressing, grilled (broiled) or stuffed and baked.

BEANS AND PEAS

High in nutritional value, these popular vegetables are available all year.

Broad (fava) beans

These beans are at their best in late spring when they are small and tender. When young they can

BELOW: Crunchy peppers are delicious in salads and stir-fries, and perfect for stuffing.

be cooked and eaten, pods and all. Cooked broad beans have a milder flavour than raw.

Green beans

French, runner and dwarf beans are eaten whole. They should be bright green and crisp. Simply top and tail and lightly cook or steam them.

Corn

Cobs of corn are best eaten soon after picking. Remove the green outer leaves and cook whole or slice off the kernels with a sharp knife. Baby corn cobs can be eaten raw, and are good in stir-fries.

THE ONION FAMILY

Onions and garlic are an absolute must in cooking and add flavour to a huge range of savoury dishes. Delicate leeks, sweet shallots and tangy spring onions (scallions) are also members of the onion family.

Onions

These strongly flavoured vegetables are an essential component of virtually all savoury vegetarian dishes. Red- or white-skinned onion varieties have a sweet, mild flavour and are good used raw in salads. Large, Spanish (Bermuda) onions are also mild and a good choice when a large quantity of onions is called for in a recipe.

Leeks

With a sweeter flavour than onions, leeks are a mainstay of the vegetarian diet. They make a perfect base for soups and stews. They are excellent braised and served with a tasty sauce.

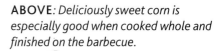

ABOVE: Deliciously sweet corn is especially good when cooked whole and finished on the barbecue.

Garlic

Used crushed, sliced or even whole, garlic develops a smooth, gentle flavour with long, slow cooking. Used raw in salads, light sauces, dressings and marindades, garlic adds a delicious, strong flavour.

MUSHROOMS

Button (white), open cup and flat mushrooms are used in vegetarian dishes all year round. Regional wild species such as ceps, chanterelles and oyster mushrooms can be found in the markets during autumn. Mushrooms can be sliced and eaten raw, dressed with a dash of extra virgin olive oil, or they can be lightly brushed with olive oil and grilled (broiled).

LETTUCES

Nutritionally, lettuce is best eaten raw, but it can be braised, steamed or made into a soup. Large-leafed varieties can be used to wrap around a filling. The cos or romaine lettuce has long, sturdy leaves and a strong flavour. Little Gem (Bibb) is a baby version of cos and has firm, densely packed leaves.

Fruit

Fruit is used extensively in vegetarian cuisine. It is used in both sweet and savoury dishes and complements both flavours well. Many fruits are naturally low in calories and fat and provide plenty of vitamin C.

ORCHARD FRUITS

Soft fruit from cultivated fruit trees grown mostly in temperate climates, these include apples, plums and pears.

Apples

There are thousands of varieties of apple, though the choice in supermakets is somewhat limited. Popular varieties include Golden and Red Delicious, Braeburn, Jonagold, Fuji, Cox's Orange Pippin, Granny Smith, Gala, and Pink Lady. The Bramley Seedling, with its thick, shiny, green skin and tart flesh, is the most familiar cooking apple and is perfect for baking, or as the basis of apple sauce.

BELOW: Apples are delicious in desserts, but also add an appealing crunch to salads.

ABOVE: *Apricots are deliciously sweet and high in fibre.*

Apricots

The best apricots are sunshine gold in colour and full of juice. They are delicious baked or used raw in salads. An apricot is at its best when truly ripe. Immature fruits are hard and tasteless and never seem to attain the right level of sweetness.

Cherries

There are two types of cherry: sweet and sour. Some are best eaten raw like the popular Bing, while others, such as Morello, are best cooked.

Choose firm, bright, glossy fruits that have fresh, green stems. Discard any that are soft, or have split or damaged skin.

Peaches and nectarines

Nectarines and peaches need plenty of sun to ripen them and are grown in Asia, the Mediterranean and North America. Peaches may be yellow-, pink- or white-fleshed, with a velvety, fuzzy skin. Nectarines are smooth-skinned, with all the luscious flavour of peaches. Peaches and nectarines are interchangeable in recipes, whether cooked or raw.

Pears

These fruit are particularly good in the late summer and autumn. Particular favourites are green and brown-skinned Conference; Williams, Comice and Packham, an excellent cooking pear.

Pears can be used in sweet and savoury vegetarian dishes; they are excellent in salads, and can be baked, poached in syrup, and used in crumbles.

Plums

Either sweet and juicy or slightly tart; plums are best cooked in desserts, or made into a delicious jam.

Plums should be just firm, and not too soft, with shiny, smooth skin that has a slight "bloom". Store ripe plums in the fridge. Unripe fruits can be kept at room temperature for a few days to ripen.

Quinces

Fragrant, knobbly fruits, with a thin, yellow or green skin. Quinces cannot be eaten raw as the seeds are poisonous. Their high pectin content makes for good jellies and, in Spain and France, quinces are used to make a fruit paste that is served with soft cheeses.

BELOW: *Pears have fine, white, granular flesh and a core containing the seeds.*

CITRUS FRUITS

Juicy, acidic and brightly coloured, citrus fruits such as oranges, grapefruit, lemons and limes are best known for their slightly bitter taste and high vitamin C content.

Oranges

Varieties of this popular fruit include seedless navel oranges, red-fleshed blood oranges and Seville (Temple) oranges. Oranges should have unblemished shiny skins and feel heavy for their size, which indicates that they contain plenty of juice and that the flesh is not dry. Choose unwaxed oranges if you intend to use the rind in recipes.

Grapefruit

The flesh of the grapefruit ranges in colour from ruby red to white; the pink and red varieties are sweeter. Served juiced, halved or cut into slices, grapefruit can provide a refreshing start to the day. The fruit also adds a refreshing tang to vegetarian salads. Cooking or grilling (broiling) mellows the tartness, but keep cooking times brief to preserve the nutrients.

BELOW: *Tangy grapefruit makes a refreshing breakfast.*

Lemons

These bright yellow citrus fruits are rich in vitamin C. They have an aromatic flavour which enhances many dishes and they are very versatile. The rind imparts a wonderful flavour to savoury vegetarian dishes, light salad dressings and desserts.

The juice can be squeezed to make a drink, or it can be added to tea, low-fat dressings and sauces. Lemons are also antioxidants, and prevent discoloration when brushed over fruits and vegetables that tend to turn brown when cut.

Limes

The juice of limes has a sharper flavour than that of lemons and if you substitute limes for lemons in a recipe, you will need to use less juice. Limes are used a great deal in Asian cooking and the rind can be used to flavour vegetarian curries, marinades and dips. Coriander, chillies, garlic and ginger are all natural partners.

BERRIES AND CURRANTS

These baubles of vivid red, purple and black are the epitome of summer and autumn, although they are now likely to be available all year round.

Strawberries

These are the favourite summer fruits and do not need any embellishment. Serve ripe and raw, on their own, or with cream and a light sprinkling sugar. Wash only if absolutely necessary and just before serving.

ABOVE: *Strawberries and raspberries are the quintessential summer fruits.*

Raspberries

Soft and fragrant, raspberries are best served raw as cooking spoils their flavour and vitamin C content. Those grown in Scotland are regarded as the best in the world. Raspberries are very fragile and require the minimum of handling, so wash only if really necessary.

Blueberries

Juicy blueberries come from the family which includes cranberries and bilberries. When ripe, the berries are plump and slightly firm, with a natural "bloom". They are sweet enough to be eaten raw (though they can be tart) but are also good cooked in muffins, used for jellies and jams, or made into a sauce to serve with nut or vegetable roasts.

BELOW: *Blueberries are packed with flavour and essential vitamins.*

RIGHT: Fresh figs go well with sweet or savoury dishes, and are a superb addition to a cheese board.

Blackberries

These are a familiar sight in early autumn, growing wild in hedgerows. Juicy and plump, blackberries can vary in sweetness, which is why they are so often cooked. Wash them carefully to prevent bruising the fruits, then pat dry with kitchen paper. Use in desserts, or make into jams and jellies.

Look for firm, glossy berries and currants. Ripe fruits generally do not keep well and are best eaten on the day of purchase – store in the refrigerator. Unripe fruits can be kept for longer.

Gooseberries

The skin of this fruit can vary from smooth and silky to fuzzy and spiky, and the flesh from the hard and sour to a sweeter, softer purple variety. Slightly unripe, tart gooseberries make wonderful crumbles or jams and jellies. Ripe, softer fruits can be puréed and mixed with yogurt or custard, to make a delicious fruit fool. A good source of vitamin A.

BELOW: Deliciously tart gooseberries.

Blackcurrants and redcurrants

These small, pretty fruits are usually sold in bunches on the stem. To remove the currants from the stalk, run the prongs of a fork down through the clusters, taking care not to damage the fruit. Wash the fruits carefully. Raw blackcurrants are quite tart, but this makes them ideal for cooking in fruit desserts such as crumbles or pies. They make delicious jams and jellies, and are especially good in summer pudding when they are partnered by other berries.

GRAPES, MELONS, DATES AND FIGS

These fruits were some of the first ever to be cultivated and are therefore steeped in history. They are available in an immense variety of shapes, colours and sizes, and with the exception of melons, they can also be bought dried.

Grapes

Fresh grapes are naturally low in fat while being rich in potassium and vitamins. Grapes tends to be heavily sprayed so you should always wash them thoroughly before consumption. Beneath the skin the flesh is always pale green and juicy. Buy bunches of grapes with fruit of equal size and not too densely packed on the stalk.

Melons

This fruit comes in many different varieties, sizes, shapes and colours, including cantaloupe, Charentais, Galia, honeydew and Ogen, which are orange- and green-fleshed varieties, and also the wonderful pink-fleshed watermelon. Ripe melons should yield to gentle pressure from your thumbs at the stalk end and have a fragrant, slightly sweet scent. If they smell highly perfumed and musky, they will probably be overripe.

Figs

Fresh figs vary in colour, from dark purple to green to a golden yellow, but all are made up of hundreds of tiny seeds, surrounded by soft pink flesh, which is perfectly edible. Choose firm, unblemished fruit that just yields to the touch. Figs are highly perishable so use quickly. Fresh figs can also be served with Greek

BELOW: Grapes add a sweet twist to salads, but are best eaten as a snack straight from the vine.

(US strained plain) yogurt and honey, or stuffed with raspberry coulis and served as a dessert. Poached in a little water or wine flavoured with cinnamon or nutmeg, they make an excellent appetizer or accompaniment.

Dates

When plump and slightly wrinkled, fresh dates have a rich honey-like flavour and dense, slightly chewy texture. They are delicious stoned (pitted) and served with Greek (US strained plain) yogurt. Dried dates can be used in the same way, but fewer are needed as the flavour is concentrated.

TROPICAL FRUIT

This exotic collection of fruits ranges from the familiar bananas and pineapples to the more unusual papayas and passion fruit.

RIGHT: Pineapples have yellow flesh that is deliciously sweet, high in fibre and loaded with vitamin C.

Pineapples

These distinctive looking fruits have a sweet, exceedingly juicy and golden flesh. Unlike most other fruits, pineapples do not ripen after picking, although leaving a slightly unripe fruit for a few days at room temperature may reduce its acidity. Choose pineapples that have fresh green spiky leaves, are heavy for their size, and are slightly soft to the touch.

Papaya

Also known as pawpaw, these pear-shaped fruits come from tropical regions. When ripe, the green skin turns a speckled yellow and the pulp is a glorious orange-pink colour. Peel off the skin using a sharp knife or a vegetable peeler before enjoying the creamy flesh which has a lovely perfumed aroma and sweet flavour.

Mangoes

The skin of these luscious, fragrant fruits can range in colour from green to yellow, orange or red. Their shape varies tremendously, too. An entirely green skin is a sign of an unripe fruit, although in Asia, these are often used in salads. Ripe fruit should yield to gentle pressure and, when cut, it should reveal a juicy, orange flesh.

Bananas

A concentrated bundle of energy, bananas are full of valuable nutrients. The soft and creamy flesh can be blended into smooth, sweet drinks, mashed and mixed with yogurt,

ABOVE: Papaya has beautiful golden flesh and is packed with edible seeds that have a peppery flavour.

or the fruits can be baked and barbecued whole.

If you wish to buy ripe bananas, choose fruits that are patched with brown. Bananas with patches of green can be ripened at room temperature.

Pomegranates

Pink, apple-shaped fruits with a tough skin, pomegranates contain hundreds of seeds covered with a deep pink flesh that has a delicate, slightly tart flavour. Try sprinkling over sweet dishes such as fruit salads. A good source of vitamin C.

BELOW: Bananas are full of energy, so are the ideal for those who need an instant boost before or after exercise.

Herbs and spices

In many vegetarian dishes, herbs and spices are added to give essential extra flavour or to enhance those already present. Flavours provided by herbs and spices contribute taste and colour, making them ideal for creating a wide range of vegetarian dishes.

RIGHT: *Rosemary and sage are traditionally used to flavour meat dishes, but their delicious aromatic fragrance makes them a welcome ingredient in the vegetarian kitchen too.*

Parsley

Both flat leaf parsley and the tightly curled variety are widely used in vegetarian cooking.

Parsley is commonly used to add flavour and colour, and it also makes an attractive garnish.

Dill

The mild, yet distinctive, aniseed flavour of dill goes well with potatoes, courgettes (zucchini) and cucumber. It makes a good addition to sauces and can be added to a wide variety of egg dishes. Add to dishes just prior to serving as its mild flavour diminishes with cooking.

BELOW: *Dill's delicate fronds and subtle aniseed flavour make it an ideal garnish for vegetable dishes.*

Bay leaves

These leaves are widely used to flavour stocks, soups and stews. They are also included in bouquet garni and can be threaded on to kebab skewers or thrown on the barbecue for flavour.

Oregano

This herb is a wild form of marjoram, and has a slightly stronger flavour. It is a very popular herb, widely used in vegetarian cooking and is a classic addition to pizza-based recipes.

Sage

The leaves of this herb, which may be silver-grey or purple, have a potent aroma and only a small amount is needed. Sage is traditionally added to meat dishes but used discreetly, it is delicious with beans, cheese, lentils and in stuffings.

Thyme

There are many types of thyme, from lemon thyme to plain garden thyme, ranging in colour from yellow to grey-green. A few sprigs will add a warm earthy flavour to vegetable soups, marinades and other vegetarian dishes.

This robustly flavoured aromatic herb is good in tomato-based recipes, and with roasted vegetables, lentils and beans. It is also essential in a bouquet garni.

Tarragon

This is a popular herb in French cooking and has an affinity with all egg- and cheese-based dishes. The short slender-leafed French variety has a warm, aniseed flavour. Tarragon also makes a zesty addition to salads and vinaigrettes.

Rosemary

Wonderfully aromatic, rosemary is traditionally used in meat dishes, but it can also add a smoky flavour to hearty bean and vegetable dishes.

LEFT: *Bay leaves are widely used to add flavour to stocks, soups and stews.*

LEFT: *Marjoram goes well with the sun-drenched flavours of the Mediterranean.*

RIGHT: *Fragrant basil and coriander are both widely-used in oriental cuisine.*

Marjoram

This herb goes well in Mediterranean-style vegetable dishes, such as ratatouille, or in casseroles and tomato sauces, but should be added at the last minute as its flavour diminishes when heated.

Coriander (cilantro)

Fresh coriander leaves impart a distinctive flavour to soups, stews, sauces and spicy dishes when added towards the end of cooking. Coriander is also used in salads and yogurt dishes.

RIGHT: *Mint has a refreshing flavour that works well in savoury dips.*

Pepper

This is one of the most versatile of all spices. Black peppercorns have the strongest flavour, which is rich, earthy and pungent. Green peppercorns are the fresh unripe berries that are bottled while soft.

Mint

Chopped mint accompanies other herbs to enhance stuffed vegetables in countries such as Greece and in countries in the Middle East. Finely chopped mint adds a cooling tang to low-fat yogurt dishes as well as teas and iced drinks.

Basil

Intensely aromatic Basil has a sweet flavour and bright green colour. The tender leaves have a natural affinity with tomatoes, aubergines (eggplants), (bell) peppers, courgettes (zucchini) and cheese. Tear the leaves rather than chop them, as they bruise easily, and add basil to dishes towards the end of the cooking time.

Cumin seeds

These dark seeds are used in Indian, Mexican, Thai and Vietnamese cuisines. Cumin has a strong, spicy, sweet aroma with a bitter, pungent taste. Cumin seeds are crushed or used whole.

Chives

A member of the onion family, chives have a milder flavour and are best used as a garnish, snipped over egg or potato dishes, or added to salads or flans.

Chillies

These small fiery relatives of the sweet (bell) pepper family and are commonly used in vegetarian cooking. Chillies, both fresh and dried, may be used in spicy vegetable stews, as well as in stir-fries, curries and other hot dishes.

BELOW: *Cumin seeds can be ground to a powder or used whole, and add an authentic flavour to spicy Indian dishes.*

BELOW: *Chillies add a fiery kick to vegetarian curries and stir-fries.*

Nutmeg

The warm aroma of nutmeg makes a good addition to many dishes, particularly those containing spinach, cheese and eggs. Buy whole nutmegs and grate them freshly as required.

Dairy products

This group of ingredients includes milk, cream, cheese and yogurt made from cow's, goat's and sheep's milk, as well as eggs. They are used in a huge range of sweet and savoury dishes, from sauces and soups to drinks and desserts.

Milk

Cow's milk remains the most popular type, although semi-skimmed (low-fat) and skimmed milks now outsell the full-fat (whole) version. Skimmed milk contains half the calories of full-fat milk and only a fraction of the fat, but nutritionally it is on a par, retaining its vitamins, calcium and other minerals.

Cream

The high fat content of cream means that it should not be eaten on a daily basis. Used with discretion, however, cream lends a richness to soups, sauces, bakes and desserts.

BELOW: *Milk and cream are an excellent source of calcium.*

LEFT: *Sour cream adds a refreshing tang to spicy dishes.*

RIGHT: *Always check that animal products have not been used in the production of a cheese before you buy it.*

Sour cream

This thick-textured cream is treated with lactic acid, which gives it its characteristic tang. It can be used in the same way as cream. Care should be taken when cooking, as it can curdle if over-heated.

Creme fraiche

This rich, cultured cream is similar to sour cream, but its high fat content, at around 35 per cent, means that it does not curdle when cooked.

Yogurt

Praised for its health-giving qualities, yogurt has earned a reputation as one of the most valuable health foods. The fat content ranges from 0.5g per 100g for very low-fat or virtually fat-free yogurts to 4g per 100g for wholemilk yogurt. The consistency may be thin or thick.

Cheese

There is a huge variety of cheese available to the vegetarian. Some, like mozzarella and feta, are more often cooked in pies or on pizzas, or used in salads, while others, like the soft, white, Camembert-type goat's cheeses, make a good addition to a cheese board.

Butter and margarine

Whether butter is better than margarine has been the focus of much debate. The taste, especially of good-quality, farmhouse butter, is certainly superior to margarine. However, butter, which contains 80 per cent saturated fat, has the ability to raise cholesterol levels in the body. Vegetable margarine contains the same amount of fat as butter, but unfortunately margarine manufacturing processes change the fats into trans fats, or hydrogenated fats. Studies have shown that trans fats may be more likely than the saturated fat in butter to damage the heart and blood vessels. In addition, cooking removes many of the health benefits of polyunsaturated fats.

Eggs

An inexpensive, self-contained source of nourishment, hen's eggs offer the cook tremendous scope, whether served simply solo or as part of a dish. There are several different types, but the best are organic, free-range eggs from a small producer.

Soya products

Soya beans are incredibly versatile and are used to make an extensive array of by-products that can be used in cooking – tofu, tempeh, textured vegetable protein, flour, miso, and a variety of sauces.

BELOW: *firm and silken tofu have different culinary uses.*

RIGHT: *Beancurd skins can be used to wrap around a wide variety of fillings.*

The soya bean is the most nutritious of all beans. Rich in high-quality protein, it is one of the few vegetarian foods that contains all eight essential amino acids that cannot be synthesized in the body and are vital for the renewal of cells and tissues.

Soya milk

This is the most widely used alternative to milk. Made from pulverized soya beans, it is suitable for both cooking and drinking and is interchangeable with cow's milk, although it has a slightly thicker consistency and a nutty flavour.

Soya cream

This is made from a higher proportion of beans than that in soya "milk", which gives it a richer flavour and thicker texture. It has a similar consistency to single cream and can be used in the same ways.

TOFU

Also known as beancurd, tofu is made in a similar way to soft cheese and there are several different types to choose from:

Firm tofu

This type of tofu is sold in blocks and can be cubed or sliced and used in vegetable stir-fries, kebabs, salads, soups and casseroles. The bland flavour of firm tofu is improved by marinating, because its porous texture readily absorbs flavours and seasonings.

Silken tofu

Soft with a silky, smooth texture, this type of tofu is ideal for use in sauces, dressings, dips and soups. It is a useful dairy-free alternative to cream, soft cheese or yogurt, and can be used to make creamy desserts.

Tempeh

Tempeh is similar to tofu but has a nuttier, more savoury flavour. It can be used in the same way as firm tofu and also benefits from marinating. While some types of tofu are regarded as a dairy replacement, the firmer texture of tempeh means that it can be used instead of meat in pies and casseroles.

Beancurd skins and sticks

Made from soya milk, dried beancurd skins and sticks have neither aroma nor flavour until they are cooked, when they will rapidly absorb the flavour of seasonings and other ingredients. They can be chopped and added to soups, stir-fries and casseroles.

TVP

Textured vegetable protein, or TVP, is a useful meat replacement and is a convenient store-cupboard item. TVP needs to be rehydrated in boiling water or vegetable stock, and can be used in stews and curries, or as a filling for pies.

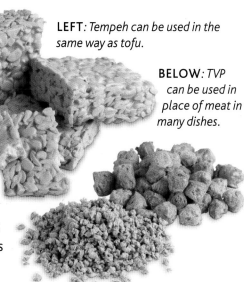

LEFT: *Tempeh can be used in the same way as tofu.*

BELOW: *TVP can be used in place of meat in many dishes.*

Pasta, rice, grains and pulses

These important staple ingredients are used as the basis of many healthy vegetarian meals. They may be added to hearty soups or vegetable stews such as tagines, used in salads such as tabbouleh, or served as accompaniments to vegetarian dishes.

PASTA

The variety of pasta shapes is almost endless, from the tiny soup pastas to huge shells used for stuffing. Low in fat and high in complex carbohydrates, pasta provides plenty of long-term energy.

Durum wheat pasta

This is the most readily available type of pasta and can be made with or without egg. Pasta made with egg has several advantages: it is more nutritious, many people consider it to have a superior flavour, and it is more difficult to overcook.

RIGHT: Flat pasta can be placed been layers of vegetables and tomato sauce to make lasagne, or rolled around a vegetable filling and topped with cheese sauce to make a vegetarian cannelloni.

Wholemeal (whole-wheat) pasta

This substantial pasta is made using wholemeal flour and it contains more fibre than plain durum wheat pasta. It has a slightly chewy texture and nutty flavour and it does takes longer to cook. There is a growing range of tempting wholemeal shapes, from tiny soup pastas to rotelle (wheels) and lasagne.

Buckwheat pasta

Pasta made from buckwheat flour has a nutty taste and is darker in colour than wholemeal (whole-wheat) pasta. Pizzoccheri is the classic shape, and is traditionally sold in nests like tagliatelle (although pizzoccheri are about half the length).

Corn pasta

This pasta is made with corn or maize flour, is gluten-free and is a good alternative for people who cannot tolerate gluten or wheat. It is made in a wide range of shapes, including spaghetti, fusilli (spirals) and conchiglie (shells).

ABOVE: Pasta comes in a variety of different shapes, sizes and colours.

Pasta shapes

From capellini (meaning 'angel hair') to thicker pasta shapes, such as fettucine, pasta comes in all sorts of shapes and sizes. As a general rule, thin spaghetti goes well with light, thin sauces, while heavier sauces mix well with the thicker tagliatelles.

Long pasta

Dried long pasta in the form of spaghetti is probably the best known, but there are many other varieties, from fine vermicelli to pappardelle. Long pasta is best served with a thin sauce, made with olive oil, butter, cream, eggs, grated cheese or chopped fresh herbs. When vegetables are added to the sauce, they should be finely chopped. Fresh spaghetti, tagliatelle and fettucine are widely available.

Short pasta

There are hundreds of different short dried pasta shapes. Short pasta isn't often sold fresh because most shapes are difficult to produce.

Conchiglie (shells) are one of the most useful shapes because they are concave and trap the sauce. Fusilli (spirals) are good with thick tomato-based sauces, farfalle (butterflies) can be served with creamy sauces, and penne (quills) go particularly well with chunky vegetable sauces.

Flat pasta

Flat pasta is designed to be baked between layers of sauce, or rolled around a filling to make cannelloni. Lasagne is made from plain or egg pasta and both fresh and dried versions are available. The pasta sheets may be flavoured with tomato or spinach, or made with wholemeal (whole-wheat) flour.

Stuffed pasta

The most common stuffed pasta shapes are ravioli, tortellini (little pies) and cappelletti (little hats). Plain, spinach and tomato doughs are the most usual, and there is a wide range of vegetarian fillings.

RICE

For over half the world's population rice is a staple food. This valuable low-fat food provides a good source of vitamins and minerals, and creates an ideal basis for a wide variety of nutritious, low-fat vegetarian dishes.

Long grain rice

The most widely used type of rice is long grain rice, where the grain is five times as long as it is wide. Long grain

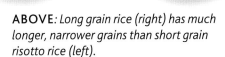

ABOVE: Long grain rice (right) has much longer, narrower grains than short grain risotto rice (left).

brown rice has had its outer husk removed, leaving the bran and germ intact, which gives it a chewy nutty flavour. It takes longer to cook than white rice but contains more fibre, vitamins and minerals.

Basmati rice

This is a slender, long grain rice, which is grown in the foothills of the Himalayas. It is aged for a year after harvest, giving it a characteristic light, fluffy texture and aromatic flavour.

Both white and brown types of basmati rice are available. Brown basmati contains more nutrients, and has a slightly nuttier flavour than the white variety.

RIGHT: Wild rice has a nutty flavour and chewy texture.

BELOW: Basmati rice is ideal for curries.

Wild rice

This is not a true rice but an aquatic grass grown in North America. It has dramatic, long, slender brown-black grains that have a nutty flavour and chewy texture. It takes longer to cook than most types of rice – from 35–60 minutes, depending on whether you like it chewy or tender. Wild rice is extremely nutritious. It contains all eight essential amino acids and is particularly rich in lysine. Use in stuffings, serve plain or mix with other rices in pilaffs and rice salads.

Risotto rice

To make Italian risotto, it is essential that you use a special, fat, short grain rice. Arborio rice, which originates from the Po Valley region in Italy, is the most widely sold variety. When cooked, most rice absorbs around three times its weight in water, but risotto rice can absorb nearly five times its weight, and the result is a creamy grain that still retains a slight bite.

BELOW: Risotto rice has short, fat grains that are highly absorbent.

OTHER GRAINS

There are other grains besides wheat and rice that provide variety in our diet and are packed with nutrients. Amongst them are oats, rye, corn, barley and quinoa. Grains come in many forms, from wholegrains to flour and are used for baking, breakfast cereals and cooked dishes.

Oats

Available rolled, flaked, as oatmeal or oatbran, oats are warming and sustaining when cooked. Whole oats are unprocessed with the nutritious bran and germ remaining intact. Oat groats are the hulled, whole kernel, while rolled oats are made from groats that have been heated and pressed flat.

Corn

We are most familiar with yellow corn or maize and in its ground form it remains an essential store-cupboard ingredient in the USA, the Caribbean and Italy.

BELOW: Oats are full of energy and make an excellent breakfast food.

LEFT: Couscous goes well with spicy dishes.

BELOW: Quinoa is a rich source of protein.

Barley

Believed to be the oldest cultivated grain, barley is a fundamental part of everyday Eastern and Asian cooking. Pearl barley, the most usual form, has a mild, sweet flavour and chewy texture, and can be added to soups, stews and bakes.

Couscous

This tiny yellowish grain is a form of pasta made from semolina. It is a staple of North African cooking and widely available in packaged form in most supermarkets. Couscous is a good source of complex carbohydrates. Couscous has a light and fluffy texture and a fairly bland flavour, which makes it a good foil for spicy dishes.

Quinoa

From the ancient Incas, this amazing grain has protein at least equivalent to that in milk and is stuffed full of potassium and riboflavin, as well as vitamin B6. Among other uses quinoa can be used in soups, salads and desserts or in pilaf recipes.

PULSES

Pulses are the edible seeds from plants belonging to the legume family.

They include chickpeas and a vast range of beans and are packed with protein, vitamins, minerals and fibre.

Lentils

These nutritious pulses come in different sizes and can be yellow, red, brown or green. The tiny green-black Puy lentils are favoured in France, whereas the brown and red ones are more popular in the Middle East, where they are often cooked with spices.

Aduki beans

These tiny, deep-red beans have a sweet, nutty flavour and are popular in Oriental dishes. In Chinese cooking, they form the base of red bean paste.

Black-eyed beans (peas)

Known as black-eyed peas in the USA, black-eyed beans are good in soups and salads, they can also be added to savoury bakes and vegetarian casseroles.

Borlotti beans

These oval beans have red-streaked, pinkish-brown skin and a bitter-sweet flavour. When cooked, they have a tender, moist texture, which is good in soups and hearty vegetable stews.

BELOW: Lentils are delicious with spices, and are a good base for a vegetarian curry.

Butter (wax) beans and lima beans

Similar in flavour and appearance, both butter beans and lima beans are characterized by their flattish, kidney shape and soft, floury texture. Cream-coloured butter beans are familiar in Britain and Greece, while lima beans are popular in the USA.

Cannellini beans

These small, white beans have a soft, creamy texture when cooked and are popular in Italian cooking. When dressed with olive oil, lemon juice, garlic and fresh chopped parsley, they make an excellent warm salad.

Chickpeas

Robust and hearty chickpeas resemble shelled hazelnuts and have a delicious nutty flavour. They need lengthy cooking and are much used in Mediterranean and Middle Eastern cooking. In India, they are known as gram and are ground into flour to make fritters and flat breads.

BELOW: Beans are tender when cooked and are an excellent addition to vegetarian stews.

Haricot (navy) beans

Most commonly used for canned baked beans, these versatile, ivory-coloured beans are small and oval in shape. Called navy or Boston beans in the USA, they suit slow-cooked dishes, such as casseroles and bakes.

Mung beans

Instantly recognizable in their sprouted form as beansprouts, mung or moong beans are small, olive-coloured beans native to India. They are soft and sweet when cooked, and are used in the spicy curry, moong dahl.

Pinto beans

The savoury-tasting pinto bean has an attractive speckled skin and features extensively in Mexican cooking, most familiarly in refried beans.

Red kidney beans

Glossy, mahogany-red kidney beans retain their colour and shape when cooked. They have a soft, "mealy" texture and are much used in South American cooking. An essential ingredient in chillies, they can also be used to make refried beans. Cooked kidney beans can be used to make a variety of salads, but they are especially good combined with red onion and chopped flat leaf parsley and mint, then tossed in an olive oil dressing.

Cooking kidney beans

Most types of beans require soaking for 5–6 hours or overnight and then boiling rapidly for 10–15 minutes to remove any harmful toxins. This is important for kidney beans, which can cause serious food poisoning if not treated this way.

1 Wash the beans well, then place in a bowl that allows plenty of room for expansion. Cover with cold water and then leave to soak overnight or for 8–12 hours, then drain and rinse.

2 Place the beans in a large pan and cover with fresh, cold water. Bring to the boil and boil rapidly for around 10–15 minutes, then reduce the heat and simmer for 30 minutes to 2 hours, until tender, depending on the type of bean. Drain and serve.

Index